REBUILDING A MAN

Fergus Farrell is a former rugby player, who won the Connacht Rugby Unsung Hero Award in 2023. A mental health and disability advocate, he is an ambassador for the Lighthouse Charity and their Make it Visible initiative. He is a proud Athenry man and a very proud father of three.

REBUILDING A MAN

MY BATTLE TO REMAKE MY BODY AND MY LIFE, AND BECOME THE MAN I WAS MEANT TO BE

FERGUS FARRELL

with LOUISE NÍ CHRÍODÁIN

Gill Books

Gill Books
Hume Avenue
Park West
Dublin 12
www.gillbooks.ie

Gill Books is an imprint of M.H. Gill and Co.

978 18045 8359 3

Design origination by O'K Graphic Design, Dublin
Typeset by Typo•glyphix, Burton-on-Trent
Edited by Jane Rogers
Proofread by Liza Costello
Printed and bound in the UK using 100% renewable electricity at CPI Group (UK) Ltd
This book is typeset in 12/18 pt Minion Pro.

The paper used in this book comes from the wood pulp of managed forests.

A CIP catalogue record for this book is available from the British Library.

5 4 3 2 1

MIX
Paper | Supporting responsible forestry
FSC® C013604

This book is dedicated to everyone who finds themselves facing adversity, or life-changing challenges, and struggles to find motivation. I hope my story will inspire you to take the first step on your own journey to recovery.

I also want to dedicate this book to the many people who have helped me since my accident in 2018, in particular those who continued to stand by me even when I did not make that easy.

Finally, this book is for my three amazing children, Aimee, Bradley and Felim. You are my own daily inspiration. Everything I do, or try to accomplish, is so that you can be proud to call me your father.

CONTENTS

1

THE ACCIDENT

The details of the day itself should be seared on my mind, but they aren't. I can't remember the weather, or what I did that morning, or the conversations I had.

I do recall how I spent my last hour as a fully able-bodied man. I'd love to turn back the clock and do it all differently, but I can't.

I was in the yard of my bus company, beside my homeplace in Athenry, County Galway, in the west of Ireland. Seán Summers, a former mechanic of mine, had bought some equipment off me and we were loading it onto his trailer. I was in my yard clothes – jeans, T-shirt and runners – and there was a bit of pulling and dragging, but it didn't take too long.

Seán hung around the yard doing a few other things, but I needed to get ready to drive a busload of players from Monivea Rugby Football Club up to Belfast to play an All-Ireland quarter-final.

In addition to running a demanding business, my wife Mandy and I were also in the process of building a new house, which I had taken on as a self-build, giving myself a lot of extra work hours and pressure. We were living in my grandmother's old house at this stage, because we had sold our own house to fund the build. That house is right beside the yard, so I went in and changed into my bus driver clothes – white shirt with our BusLink brand, black tie, black pants – to look clean and tidy.

I went back to the office and realised I had 15 or 20 minutes to spare. I could have sat down and had a cup of coffee and a chat with someone, relaxed for a few minutes, but I didn't – that was the way my life had become. I spotted a rusty steel bench over in the corner of the yard, and I thought, 'Someone's going to hit that; it needs to be moved.' It weighed about 70kg, and normally – if I'd had my yard clothes on – I would have grabbed it on either side and duck-walked with it. But I didn't want to get my clothes dirty, so I called out to Seán, 'Come on, we'll move this because someone is going to reverse into it at night and damage one of the buses.'

We picked up the bench, and I lifted it away from my body – I didn't want to get rust on my clothes. We had only walked about ten steps when I felt a terrible pain, a dart, in my back, and I had to drop it.

As I dropped the bench, it felt like an electric shock was running up through my spine, up through my back. However, the bench was now in the middle of the yard, and it had to be moved. After taking a few minutes to recover – being a typical man and wanting to show no pain, no weakness – I said, 'C'mon, Seán, we'll move this.' It was the worst decision I ever made. Once again I lifted it out from my body. I took one step, and bang! It all happened in a split second, a click of the fingers. It was as if someone had put a shotgun to the middle of my back and pulled the trigger; I felt a massive explosion in my back, and I collapsed to the ground.

The bench fell hard on top of me, trapping my legs underneath. I was roaring in pain but I couldn't feel the weight of the bench; I couldn't feel my legs. I could see them, but they didn't feel connected to me any more. I didn't know what was going on, just that I was engulfed in pain, bellowing in agony.

I don't know how long it was, maybe a couple of minutes, before I could catch my breath. There was a belt around my waist and it felt as if it was melting into my skin. I was trying to get it off but it seemed to take ages, and it was a mammoth effort. Even when I pulled it off, the pressure I felt wasn't relieved. It seemed like every last bit of my lower body was burning, as if there was plastic melting into my skin. I still hadn't realised that I had lost all power from the belly button down, and that fiery sensation was all my nerve endings, hundreds of thousands of them, trying to reconnect. But they couldn't reconnect because my spinal cord had been almost completely severed.

In between roaring I shouted at Seán to get my wife Mandy, who was in the house. Mandy is a nurse, a midwife, and she knew we needed to call the paramedics immediately.

I was meant to be in the bus driving to pick up the team at this stage, and, despite the pain, my main concern was making sure the job got done. I managed to gather enough breath to divert Ian, another driver who was in the yard, to do the job: 'Can you go to Belfast?' That's how my mind worked back then; everything was focused on work, on the business. It was ridiculous when I look back at it.

Other people came into the yard but I don't remember much more. I think they had the bench lifted off me before the paramedics arrived, but I couldn't move.

The paramedics drove into the yard after about 30 or 40 minutes, led by Tommy Maughan. Like almost everyone I would meet in the HSE, they were brilliant. They put a compression suit around me and started giving me the green whistle – an inhaled pain relief medication called Methoxyflurane – for pain relief. But it made no difference.

It took about half an hour to assess me, to put that compression suit on, and to get me into the ambulance. Tommy was talking to me all the time, but as we were getting nearer Galway there was still no movement, no power in my legs, and the pain was horrific.

The paramedics got me seen quickly. The hospital organised an MRI scan, and I remember the nurses trying to move me from the trolley to the machine. It was agony. I was screaming 'Stop, stop!' I just couldn't tolerate it and they started getting angry with me. Eventually they got me on, but an MRI machine is a hard surface, and I had to stay still for 40 minutes. I think it was one of the hardest things I've ever had to endure.

It was then the alarm bells started ringing. I know now that the radiologist reported '*a large central disc herniation at T9–10 with mass effect on the cord and stenosis of the right exit foramen at this level*'. An orthopaedic surgeon, Mr Emmet Cullen, was called, even though he was off duty. He told me, 'Okay, we have a twelve-hour window. You're in trouble here. You have a severe back injury. We don't have the expertise here to operate and we'll have to get you to Dublin.'

There were people coming and going. I was hooked up to IVs and they were putting stuff into my veins. My wife and my parents were there at this stage, and you could just see how worried they were, especially Mandy.

The hospital rang the Mater Hospital, which houses the National Spinal Injuries Unit, but they didn't have space for me, so then they rang Beaumont Hospital, also in Dublin. As arrangements were being made with Beaumont, the Mater rang back and said they could take me. I was to be airlifted by helicopter because I needed to be operated on straight away, but they wanted another MRI first, to give them a clearer picture of what was going on. So I had to go through the ordeal of an MRI again. It was excruciating, but at least I knew what to expect this time. But because of the delay in getting that MRI, it was now dark, and the helicopter that had come down to bring me to Dublin couldn't fly at night.

They blue-lighted me to Dublin in an ambulance. Because I was a bus driver I knew every inch of that motorway. I knew exactly how long it would take. There was an older paramedic in the ambulance, a lovely man, but he kept leaning over me telling me, 'You'll be fine. You'll be fine. I had a back injury before myself, and look, I'm flying.' And all I was thinking was 'Would you ever fuck off.' He was only trying to be good to me, but every vibration in that vehicle amplified the excruciating pain running up through my back. For that entire journey it felt as if I had my hand on an electric fence. It was shock after shock after shock. I could think of nothing else.

We eventually arrived at the Mater, and at first it didn't seem that they were expecting us. They even had to clear out a room for me, and all this time I could think about nothing but the pain. They started telling me things, but it was all a blur. All I knew was I had to get an operation. It had to be done. It was going to take eight or nine hours, and I had to sign the consent form. I just said, 'Do it!'

As I was being prepared for the operation, which was to be led by Ms Noelle Cassidy, I realised the anaesthetist was from Barna in Galway, and I was so happy to see another Galwegian. But then came my first realisation of exactly where my life had led me. She weighed me so that she could calculate how much drugs she had to administer to knock me out for up to nine hours, and I was 123kg. At 39 years of age I was morbidly obese, and I hadn't even realised it.

Ignorance is bliss. I'm glad I didn't know what was ahead of me as I waited to be put under. I went into that operation thinking, 'When I come out, the pain will be reduced, and I might have movement. I might have feeling in my legs.'

WHY I'VE WRITTEN THIS BOOK.

I'm hoping that my experiences can inspire others on their own toughest trek, to help them see life from a new perspective, to show that it's within all of us to overcome adversity, that every challenge we are faced with is an opportunity to grow, that every day offers a fresh opportunity to improve ourselves.

The messages at the end of each chapter highlight some of the lessons I have learned, and what I wish I'd known when I was younger.

If I could turn back time I would tell younger me to take better care of himself and those around him. I would tell myself to get my head out of the clouds, and look at everything good I already had in my life; to stop always trying to keep up with the Joneses. I would tell myself that debt is a form of modern slavery, and to stop putting pressure on myself to grow a bigger and better business. I would tell myself that real success is when you have time and patience for your loved ones. I would tell myself to enjoy my life and the people in my life, and that there should never not be time to take ten minutes out to relax and enjoy a chat, or rest up.

2

AFTER THE OPERATION

The moment I woke up after the operation remains vividly imprinted on my memory. I was lying on my back in the hospital bed. My feet were propped up on a plinth in front of me, splayed out and falling to the side. They were a perfect frame for the windows in the room that looked out into the nurses' station. However, though I could see them in front of me, I couldn't feel them. I couldn't move them. They didn't even feel like they belonged to me. It was as if someone else's feet had been put into the bed with me, and my own had gone missing. The pain was even worse than it had been when I was last conscious; intense post-operative pain had now been added to the mix.

You can see from my initial MRI scan that my spinal cord had been cut but not completely severed. It was hanging on by a thread; that's why I had needed the operation within 12 hours. The T9 and T10 discs, in the middle of the spine, were ruptured. The fluid inside the T10 disc was leaking out, and this is what had damaged the cord. The surgeons wouldn't ever touch the spinal cord, so as far as I could understand what they had done was remove some of the discs (a discectomy) and insert a cage around the area to restore spine stability.

I seemed to have wires hanging out of me everywhere, attached to whirring and beeping machines on both sides of me. When I turned my head I could see at least one intravenous (IV) drip, which was plugged into a cannula in my hand. Suddenly my stomach sank as I realised I also couldn't feel my right arm. Could it actually be even worse than I'd thought? I was so relieved when they told me that the numbness had been caused by pinched nerves from lying on the operating table for hours. The feeling in my arms returned within a couple of days.

From the moment I awoke my timelines became jumbled – probably a combination of anaesthesia and drugs – and I am sure I was groggy and drifting in and out of consciousness. However, it did seem I had been lying there for a while when the assistant surgeon came in, sat down beside me, and began talking. I wasn't taking in what he was saying. I was in my own world, just staring at my legs, or through that window, thinking, 'I'm in serious trouble here.' I do recall him asking if I had any questions, and I looked at my legs and looked up at him and asked, 'Is this the way I'm going to be?' He turned his face towards mine, put his hand on my shoulder and said, 'Sorry, Fergus. You have been very, very, unlucky.' And then he got up and walked out.

I'm a very traditional type of man. My daughter was only seven at the time, but my first thought after he left was, 'I'm never gonna walk Aimee down the aisle.' And then my mind turned to my five-year-old son, and I thought, 'I'll never play soccer with Bradley out the back of our new home.'

It was a while before I even remembered our seven-month-old son, Felim. And this was the second realisation of where my life had led me, where my obsession with business had taken me. I hadn't thought about Felim because I hadn't taken the time to build a relationship with him. I had let the business become more important than my infant son. I had been so busy with everything else in my life – business, employees, managing finances – that I hadn't had time to develop that bond.

That realisation really hit me hard. I was disgusted with myself, and to this day it bothers me. What an awful way I had been living my life. On the outside I had it all: a big business; a nice family; a good car; a new house under construction. However, I had no relationship with my baby son. That was a horrible recognition.

At this stage 24 hours hadn't passed since the accident, and my family, who had followed me to Dublin, were also trying to get to grips with what had happened. Mandy came in to be with me, and though I wasn't fully awake and aware, I could still recognise the anguish and worry in her face. She obviously knew more about my prognosis than I did, and was anxious and upset for me, and about what the future held.

On my own again, I began to recognise the routine. Every couple of hours two nurses' aides – amazing men – would come in and move me, so I wouldn't get bedsores. They would move me from my back onto one shoulder, and then onto my back again, then onto my other shoulder, and then onto my back again. That was how I spent that second night in the Mater – and many nights after. But even if I hadn't been constantly disturbed, I couldn't have slept with the pain. It was still horrendous.

Amidst the pain my mind was starting to process what had happened, and what might lie ahead. Seeing the fear in Mandy's eyes had made me realise I hadn't time for self-pity. If I was feeling sorry for myself up in Dublin, that would put pressure on people at home in Athenry, my family, my friends, my employees. If I ever saw someone upset or struggling, it always made me feel bad.

While I had been in Accident & Emergency my best mate, Paul Neary, had rung me. His wife had just given birth to a new baby the night before and he was delighted. I didn't want to spoil his big day so I never let on what condition I was in. What I found out recently is that Mandy texted him afterwards to let him know that I was in a bad way. But that's where my head was always at, not wanting to worry other people, and my mindset lying in that hospital bed was no different.

So I decided that I could at least try and alleviate some of the worries about me. The only way I could do that was by becoming the most positive-minded spinal cord injury patient the Mater had ever seen. If I could make them think that I was happily getting on with everything, they could leave me in Dublin and get on with their everyday lives.

That was my first good decision.

* * *

You don't get fit by just thinking about it. So, as I lay there, with machines beeping all around me, I started figuring out how I could make myself, and keep myself, positive. I knew that positivity could actually generate endorphins and help my body cope.

I probably got about an hour's sleep that first night between the pain, the disruptions and my racing mind. The next day the same surgeon came back in and we had a long chat. It was the first time I recall being told what had actually happened to me. He explained that I had ruptured thoracic discs in my spine, and that one (the T10) had gone through my spinal cord and severed – 'pinched' is the word the medics use – it by up to 90 per cent.

Although my spinal cord had not been completely severed, mine was considered a T11 ASIA Impairment Scale A spinal cord injury, which means paralysed for life from the belly button down, with virtually no prospect of getting any movement back. He laid out the statistics, and they were stark. 'If you get movement 72 hours after the operation, you have a five per cent chance of gaining some sort of strength or movement.' He didn't say 'walking', just 'some sort' of strength. And after 72 hours? My percentage chance dropped to zero per cent! That was my prognosis. It was devastating.

There were visitors, including my sister Attracta, and lots of nursing activity. I was catheterised, wearing a nappy, being washed down. I could do nothing for myself. Every two hours people came in to move me from one side to another. My legs were still up on the plinth. I was completely reliant on the nurses and aides. I just felt useless. And though I don't think I thought of the word dependent at the time, I was utterly dependent.

I knew I couldn't lie there and not do anything for myself, so I started thinking about how I could use a tool I have turned to all my life – visualisation.

Long before I knew there was a name for it, I had used visualisation. When I was a kid and wanted to play sports, I visualised myself going around in the Irish jersey. I was a young laddeen during the 1995 World Cup and Jonah Lomu's seven tries for the All Blacks. I would visualise myself running down a pitch with the ball, just like him. I would go out into the front garden with a rugby ball tucked under my arm, and race backwards and forwards, shimmying between the trees, imagining they were other players and I was side-stepping them.

That visualisation technique would help me improve my rugby; and when I was grown up and in business, I visualised buying my first new bus. However, I never visualised something that wasn't in my power to achieve. I only visualise things I can impact. I've never visualised being up in Lotto HQ with the big cheque, and there's no point in visualising yourself in the green jersey of Ireland if you're not going to work to earn it.

As soon as I had time to myself, I started visualising. I knew I was going to have to start small. Start small and build, was my thinking. I didn't picture myself jumping up and walking out the door. That was something I knew could never happen. I visualised myself moving my big right toe, making a small movement with my big toe. I don't know why I decided to focus on that toe, but I did.

There was a circuit board behind me on the wall, a switch on the wall in front of me and a light overhead. I started visualising that my brain was a circuit board, and I needed to make a connection between my brain and my toe through my broken spinal cord, to move my toe, flick the switch and turn on that light.

I imagined setting off a spark of in my brain – like you would if you tried to create a spark with a flint on stone. That lit a fuse, and that fuse lit a wire which fizzled right down through my body; sending that spark down through my neck, my broken spinal cord, my groin, my leg, until it finally hit my right big toe. And when the spark hit my toe it would make it move and push the switch, to turn on the light.

That's what I kept visualising. This was my time to fight, to fight for myself. I blanked everything else out, and in the following days every time I was on my own I visualised that spark moving my big toe.

I visualised that tiny movement hundreds of times. In my mind I would follow that wire down through my body and into my toe … and every time I did it I would add more detail.

I think the 72 hours were up at around five or six in the morning. I was on my own. I concentrated and started visualising. I stared at my toe, willing it to even twitch. Nothing happened. I tried it again, and again, and again. Nothing happened. My 72 hours were up and I had no movement below my waist. I had been told my chances of regaining any movement or strength were now zero. Despite all the drugs, that hit hard.

CHOOSE POSITIVITY.

Finding a way to stay positive is key, as a positive mindset really can help lift your spirits. My injury was the worst I was going to get. It was my choice to stay positive for those around me, and to try to improve, to try to get better, no matter how tiny those improvements were going to be.

3

MY BIG TOE

When I realised the visualisation hadn't worked, I didn't stop. I just kept on doing it. I knew there was no point lying there feeling sorry for myself, and I needed to stay as positive as I could. It's a lot easier to stay positive when you can see some progress. But I had always also used other people's negativity as a driver. If I'm told I can't do something, that makes me want to do it more. Visualising that big toe moving gave me a purpose. It gave me something to work on, something to occupy my mind. I never gave up on myself. I told myself, 'If you stop, there's no chance.'

It's like going out on the rugby pitch. If you don't train for it, you're going to get smashed. If you train, you'll dominate. I viewed that visualisation as another form of training. My parents had always instilled in me that hard work equals rewards. There is no substitute for hard work. Continuing with the visualisation, continuing to picture that wire connecting my brain to my big toe and turning on the light switch, was my way of putting in the yards. I had just been told that I had zero per cent chance of movement, but lying there and doing nothing just wasn't in my DNA. It was also a diversion from thinking about the pain, which was still preventing me from sleeping. The only time I dozed briefly was when I tapped the morphine drip and it gave me another dose, or if I drifted off from pure exhaustion.

My feet constantly felt like they were on fire, that they were burning. I wanted to put ice blocks on them. There was a lovely nurse – I have forgotten her name but I do recall her red hair – and I always felt she really understood what her patients were going through. I asked her if there was anything that might help, and she came in and massaged my feet. It didn't relieve the pain, but it did dampen the burning sensation. It was like the best drug ever, just an incredible feeling. I remember thinking, if I had the money, I would have somebody massage my feet all day long, every day. In all that agony and pain that act of kindness was a respite. I could see her at my feet, I could see her massaging my feet but I couldn't feel her touch my toes. However, I could feel the tingles up in my neck. I can feel that sensation even now when I'm thinking about it.

I had been transferred to another room, and about day five or six they got a hoist to lift me up out of the bed and put me in a wheelchair. There's a photo of me in the chair and I look huge, but that was a good moment. However, it now seemed like everything was getting harder. Even breathing seemed a chore. I tried to explain for a couple of days that I was finding it tougher going than usual, that I was feeling more unwell. Nothing must have been apparent, but when Mandy came in to see me one morning – she and the kids had been staying at a friend's house – and I told her I was struggling to breathe, within minutes there were people all around me.

They brought a machine to X-ray my chest and it turned out I had two massive clots in my lungs. So for a couple of days there were people by my side constantly, giving me medications and carrying out procedures. It was a very frightening time, even more than the accident, because I could see the panic around me; and I knew Mandy was really worried. However, I came through that. It wasn't my time.

One of my visitors at the Mater was rehabilitation consultant Dr Éimear Smith, the medical director at the National Rehabilitation Hospital (NRH) in Dún Laoghaire, and she agreed I was a candidate for spinal cord injury rehabilitation. However, there was a 16- to 18-week waiting list for a bed. So when I had recovered from the clots on my lungs, I got the news that I was being transferred to St Finbar's Ward at Galway University Hospital. It was brilliant news because now I would be able to see more of Mandy, my kids, my family and friends. But I was also filled with dread at the thought of the two and a half-hour ambulance journey. If it was anything like the journey coming up to Dublin, I really didn't want to go, but I had no option. Luckily the journey wasn't as horrendous as the first, but it was still very difficult. The engine's vibrations sent constant waves of pain through my spine.

I arrived at St Finbar's late in the evening of 6 November. They seemed to be unaware of just how paralysed and just how heavy I was, because when they were transferring me from the ambulance bed to the ward bed, they let me fall between the two. I laugh about it now but, man, was I angry at the time. When I was on that floor, it was a mission to get me up because I was a deadweight. It was that moment, lying there helpless, that brought home very quickly just how dependent I now was on others.

However, once I got over that it was a great place to be. Everyone was lovely and one of the nurses was Martina Finnerty, who went to school across the road from my school. It was so good to see a familiar friendly face.

A few days into my stay there was another issue. I had been getting spasms in my legs since after the operation – I still get them – but suddenly, totally out of the blue, my body started going into massive convulsions. I knew they were happening but I couldn't do anything about it. Once again that was extremely frightening, with doctors and nurses coming and going until they got it sorted, and it took them a while. I could also sense a nervousness about my condition, and that was frightening too.

Afterwards, when I had time to reflect, I realised I had almost become accustomed to having no power in my legs, but the other health battles were really getting to me. I wondered if this was the normal life of a person who is paralysed, and what I could expect; constant worries about lung clots and seizures, and not knowing what was coming next. It was an overwhelming thought.

It was hard to stay positive and fight through that, but I settled into St Finbar's and I started visualising again, as much as I could. I was still catheterised and still had a nappy on; I had no control over my bowel and my bladder. One day Ireland was playing the All Blacks and my good friend Noel Rabbitte came in to watch the match. During the game my bowels released. Noel said nothing. He just stayed and watched with me. I don't know how he stuck it. Now that's a friend!

When I was in the Mater only really close friends and family had come to visit because I was in such a bad way. But back in Galway, so many friends went out of their way to see me, including old school friends and people from the rugby community. John Cooke, my rugby mentor and a former employer, came to visit me the day before he was due to move to India. He came with Pat

Devane, another fella I played rugby with, who I had visited many years before in St Finbar's when he almost lost his arm in a shotgun accident. Johnny saw me at the stage where I had to be hoisted to be moved, and he would follow my journey from India. He is always a very positive man, and he told me later that when he was leaving the hospital, he thought to himself, 'Fergus has a hell of a battle ahead of him, but if any lad is going to do it, he will.'

When my back had healed after the operation I was shown how to lift myself up using a triangle that was suspended over my head and attached to the back of the bed. Our core is what holds us up; those muscles in our torso that stabilise our spine and pelvis. My core no longer had any strength. My centre of gravity was gone. I couldn't hold myself up even in a sitting position.

Getting even a little bit of stability back, to be able to hold my upper body steady while sitting up in bed, was a meticulous, methodical and painstaking process. It started with me being supported as I lifted one hand off the bed for a split second, and then the other. I would be shaking with the effort. Eventually I progressed to keeping a hand off the bed for a second longer, and then a couple of seconds, without falling forward or back. Finally I gained a bit of confidence and would lean forward a little bit further to stay sitting upright. I kept making tiny progressions. Soon I was able to move myself around quite freely in bed, because I had good upper body strength. I used the triangle to lift myself up and move myself from left to right.

The next stage was to sit me up at the side of the bed. My legs were dangling over the edge – I could see them but they didn't feel part of me. Once again I braced myself with both hands down on the mattress. If I let go I would just fall backwards, so two staff held on to me, one on either side, while I lifted one hand for a split second, and then the other. They would try this once or twice, but I always wanted to do more and more, though it was exhausting to do even the simplest things. The sweat would pour off me from the effort and exertion. Eventually I could sit on the side of the bed without falling backwards. Each tiny gain, each minute improvement, was followed by another tiny gain, another minute improvement. It was building me back up.

The staff were always trying to get me to do things, to get me to try to understand that even though my legs were paralysed, even though I didn't have movement, my legs were still there, they still belonged to me, even though my brain couldn't feel any connection. So when I was confident sitting on the side of the bed without using my hands as anchors, they put my feet on the ground, and told me to let go.

Despite being held on to, one of the most frightening things I have ever had to do in my life was to sit up on the side of a bed, put my feet on the ground, and lift my hands off the mattress. They were trying to show me that I could still use my legs as an anchor, that I could have my feet on the ground and they would hold me. I had to start thinking about them as if they were two crutches I could lean on. It sounds easy, but when you can't feel your feet, when your mind doesn't believe there's anything there, anything bearing your weight, it is terrifying.

It was scary, but I eventually did let go out for a second, and gradually I twigged that I could use other parts of my body, and that I needed to work with them. I progressed very slowly to standing on my feet, holding on to the bed. But my legs were just anchors. They couldn't move. I had no control.

All that happened within ten days of getting to St Finbar's, and then they started to teach me how to get from the bed to the wheelchair, and from the wheelchair back onto the bed, or onto the commode. Prior to this they would bring a commode in beside me and hoist me on. They would come in around 6.30 a.m., give me a suppository, come back an hour or two later, and hoist me on to the commode to go to the toilet. I would be left there for about an hour, and then they could come back, hoist me off and clean me up.

I started to get wheeled down to the physiotherapy room. The guys there were brilliant. One of the first things they did was strap me into a plinth that rotated upwards to put me into a standing position. This was to help maintain muscle mass and bone density by putting weight down through my body. On the first day they raised me up by 45 degrees, the next day it was 60 degrees, and the next day maybe 90 degrees. It was actually quite cool.

They began helping me to adjust to the change in my centre of gravity. They got me to hold myself up on the handrails, using my arms because I had good upper body strength. I thought my legs were moving at one stage, but they were just swinging because I was taking the weight off them. However, it was a strange but wonderful feeling to be upright again. The effort that was involved in using the handrails was absolutely insane. After the session I would be totally exhausted, but then I'd be taken to the occupational therapy room, and there was a woman there who really knew how to push me, getting me to pull myself up from my wheelchair by using a kitchen sink.

I still had zero control, zero connection with my lower body. However, everything I did counted because it kept my body active, and my legs active, and the muscles active, even though there was no correspondence between what was in my head and what was happening down below. It was all involuntary. When I pulled myself up my legs were just moving with my body like a puppet on strings.

While all this was going on, business had to be dealt with. One of our biggest customers, Trafalgar, the tour company, asked me to take a video phone call to tell them how I was going to control my business, knowing that I was paralysed and in hospital. I had to go out into the corridor to take this video call, to tell them I had great people in place managing the day-to-day operations. However, about half an hour later I received an email from them cancelling the contract, a contract which was worth about €1.2 million. They were entirely within their contractual rights but we had lost a huge contract overnight the previous year, so this was another massive body blow.

That was another pressure on me, but I tried not to let it affect me because I had progressed physically. Mentally, I was showing a very positive face but there was a lot going in the background – a lot.

Losing that huge contract with Trafalgar gave me the first opportunity to park the business and concentrate on me. I knew every bit of progress I made, every improvement, was going to make life easier for the people around me when I got out. Whether that was moving one toe, or all ten toes, any improvement was going to make life easier for whoever was going to have to care for me. That was my mindset, and everything else took a back seat. But my business problems were still preying on my mind.

I was taking so many different types of drugs that I usually couldn't sleep at night, so I would do my visualisation, watch something on my laptop to distract myself from the pain and worries, and eventually drift off for an hour. Then the pain would wake me up and I would start visualising again. About 21 days after the accident, I was watching something around 2.30 a.m. and I decided to stop and do some visualisation. I was looking down at my big toe, when suddenly something seemed different. Something felt different. I'd say my heart skipped a beat. I thought, 'I'm after moving that big right toe!' And I did it again. But then I began to wonder if I was hallucinating or if it had actually moved.

Gary, the aide who came in early every morning to look after me, wasn't due for another four hours. During those hours I had myself driven cracked trying to figure out if the toe was moving or not. When he finally arrived I couldn't wait to get the words out: 'Gary, Gary, I'm after moving my big toe!'

I was exhausted at this stage and emotionally drained, but I tried again to move my toe to show him. 'That's after moving. It moved,' he confirmed. Now when I say 'move' I mean the tiniest flicker of motion, barely millimetres. But it did move under my control. I had spasms that moved my feet and legs all the time, but this movement was under my control. I wasn't hallucinating.

Gary was thrilled for me and very excited. He went off to get the nurse who was coming on duty to tell her 'Fergus has moved!', and she came in and saw the toe moving too. She was delighted for me. She knew how much that tiny movement meant, and she told me the consultant, Dr Cullen, would come in at the start of his rounds – he usually came to me at the end of his rounds.

So Dr Cullen came in with his entourage. 'Fergus, I heard you might have movement. Show me.' There was a big crowd around me, so I visualised again and eventually I moved my toe. And he said 'Okay', but his next words were like cold water: 'Now, Fergus. These could be involuntary spasms.' But he asked me to try it again, and I did, and it moved. And he said 'do it one more time', and eventually I did; once again there was a tiny movement. Dr Cullen stood back and said, 'That's most unexpected.' I just went, 'Fuck yeah!' I felt a massive release and a surge of hope, even though I was mentally, physically and emotionally drained from the effort.

That tiny flicker was the first movement I had controlled in my lower body since my accident. That minuscule movement was an improvement, a gain, and once you have a gain it's very easy to keep driving yourself. I had progress. My old foundations had collapsed, but I had now begun laying down the new foundations I needed.

The news about my big toe spread fairly quickly, and suddenly I was told my wait time for the NRH had been slashed. Because I had got some movement, they would start working with me immediately.

Within a few days I was on my way. I had no idea of what lay ahead. I was excited about the possibility of regaining more movement in my lower limbs. I was nervous too, very nervous. But I knew that whatever was to come I would have to be determined, just as I always had been, just as my parents had taught me to be.

TAKE IT STEP BY STEP.

The minuscule movement of my big toe was an improvement, a massive gain, and once you have a gain it's very easy to keep driving yourself. It can be a slow process but if you just take it step by step you will be amazed where that can eventually bring you.

4

THE FIELDS OF ATHENRY

I was born in June 1979. I had a lovely upbringing, a great childhood. I grew up just outside Athenry town in County Galway. The place is called Rockfield Cross, and it's well named; dig six inches into the fields around our house and you will hit rock.

Our house was in a dip between two straight stretches on the Craughwell Road, and when we were younger we used to play out on that road. You couldn't now; it's just too busy. It was typical of the four-bedroom box bungalows that were built around Ireland in the 1970s and early '80s. My older sister Attracta and I had identical bedrooms.

My mother, Peggy Folan, a hardy but quiet woman, was from Carna in Connemara. My father, Philip, had grown up in the neighbouring house over the wall, which had been a two-roomed cottage when he was young. My grandmother still lived there with my cousin Derek.

Both my grandparents on my father's side had been reared just down the road. My grandmother was a tough cookie, a lovely woman who raised five children. My grandfather worked as a builder and carpenter but he died when he was only 52. I never met him. He built the house his family lived in, and my father built ours, with the help of Derek's father, Peter Caulfield, and a few others.

We had about five acres around us, including a big front garden with trees. You couldn't grow anything on the land. It was filled with ferns, and we used to make trails through them and play hide and seek.

Both my parents were extremely hard-working. Dad was a farmer. He had a fruit and veg shop in Athenry, and also sold from market stalls. We had a big shed out the back where he kept supplies and deliveries of eggs and other things to sell. However, his farm was about a mile away. He grew seasonal vegetables, the usual Irish fare of potatoes, carrots, parsnips, turnips, cabbages, onions, scallions and rhubarb. He would also head into Galway city, fill up the van with tomatoes, apples and other stuff he didn't grow, and drive out to Connemara every Monday and Thursday to sell to shops and restaurants. Attracta and I would wait up for him to come home during the winter months, because he always brought us back a treat of a can of Lilt and a Toffee Crisp.

The fact that one of the other few core childhood memories I recall is about vehicles might be a hint of where my interests lay from a young age. I can still picture two new vehicles my dad bought: 89 G 391, a Ford Transit van for the vegetables; and 89 G 392, a gorgeous blue Ford Sierra, which also looked like a garda car, because the force was using a lot of those cars at the time.

About once a month Mum would drive Attracta and me out to see Nanny, her mother, in that Ford Sierra, a drive of at least an hour and a half. Nanny lived out in Moyrus in Carna, an isolated but beautiful place in the Gaeltacht. When we arrived she would be taking homemade scones out of her old range. They would let out steam when we cut them open and we would cover them with butter and jam and eat them with cups of tea. Later she would cook up a big piece of steak – a huge luxury back then – and it would be served with her own floury Kerr Pink potatoes (she grew all her vegetables) topped with a lump of butter and salt. Her food was just heaven. I would just eat and eat because it was so good.

When we'd eaten we'd wander around the fields. The landscape was so different from Athenry. We'd walk along the stone walls, or head down to what we called Nanny's beach, about 500 metres away down a boreen. It was, and is, a stunning beach, and probably remains, despite all the travelling I have done, my favourite place in the world. It's always quiet, and a place I really love going back to. You look across to a hill on an island, which hides a view of Roundstone, and in the distance you can see the Twelve Pins and the Maamturk Mountains. Behind it there's a ruined church and a cemetery, where Nanny is now buried, God rest her soul, with my grandfather, Mark, who I never met, and her son, Anthony.

I look like my dad, but I'm a larger man. Apparently I take after my late uncle Jock, who was known as a big strong man, and who moved to England. However, I was actually born underweight, and to build me up, for nourishment, my mother would mix eggs into the milk in my bottle. I don't know if it's coincidence but ever since I can remember I've hated everything to do with eggs, the smell of them, even the look of them.

However, I ate all around me from the age of about four or five. Because my dad sold fruit and veg we had any amount of them, and I would eat plates of spuds with lumps of butter. The meat didn't matter so much, but it was most often bacon and cabbage or spare ribs. I ate as much fruit as I could get my hands on, and when my dad had a shop in town that sold sweets, I think I ate a lot of his stock! Even nowadays I have to watch the amount of sweets I eat, particularly if I'm not busy, or if I'm tired. My mother always served up home-cooked meals. The food was simple, and we loved it. We'd come home from school to corned beef sandwiches and oxtail soup, my favourite.

By the age of about eight, I would have given a hand with the shop or the stall before school. At weekends I might help pick cabbages, bag turnips, pull carrots or pick potatoes. In the summer I might build stone walls or put up fences. I got a few pence or a pound for helping out, but getting up at 7 a.m. – sometimes 5 a.m. – no matter what the weather was, definitely helped toughen me up. It taught me that no matter what it is like outside, you get up and get on with work; and after the hard work you get your reward.

One summer Dad got in two or three trailer-loads of turnips, a mountain of turnips that filled a shed almost to the roof. He handed machete knives to myself, Derek and another cousin, Paddy Farrell, to cut the tops off all the turnips and bag them up. There were no health and safety concerns back then. I was only about eight or nine, so I probably wasn't much use, but we got through it. There were no thanks, but we did get paid something for the work.

People often ask me how you build resilience in a teenager. Well, I'm not very fond of the word 'resilience', but I believe that resilience is built from your life, and that I am more driven and determined because of my upbringing, because I had to do these things. So when I knew there was hard work to be done to get back up on my feet, I wasn't afraid of that hard work. Do you call that resilience? I don't. I call that understanding what hard work is.

We always had dogs and cats, and they would have the run of the house. All of us love animals, and there are still usually a few underfoot around all our homes, looking for attention. Apparently I even had a 'pet' bull, George, that I would hang out with. But I didn't enjoy working with livestock when we had them, because Dad would be in one corner of a field shouting at me to run here, and run there, and then curse at me if I let the cattle escape out the gate. I did like the beef nuts that we kept for feed. I'd say I was about eight or nine when I started popping into the shed on my way to school, grabbing a fist full of the nuts, sticking them in my pocket and eating them like little treats throughout the day. I looked up the ingredients of some modern cattle nuts and they contain maize, barley, minerals, vitamins, trace elements and about 15–16 per cent protein, so I suppose you could say I was getting a daily multivitamin supplement!

I much preferred selling fruit and veg from stalls than working with the livestock. We sold in towns like Ennis, Mountbellew, Claremorris, Athenry. I loved chatting with people, and doing a bit of bartering, making deals. And it made me very good at maths. Even at seven or eight years of age I could work out how much six apples, a cabbage and six oranges were, and then figure out the change. There were no calculators. When we had quizzes in school and there were maths questions I would usually be the first to answer. The teacher would call out sums and I would be adding it in my head as they were talking; everyone else was writing it down and adding it up. Working on the stall also gave me my ease with talking to people. It gave me great life skills.

The stalls also gave me opportunities to eat more. Martin Lynch had a takeaway on the square in Athenry, and I started putting chips and burgers on credit – on a tab! I think Dad had to go in and settle up with him every now and again, and sometimes there might be a trade for a bag of onions. We often went to Ennis on Saturdays as there was a big market there. When I had worked for a while Dad would give me a few pounds – work for reward. I would go up the town to buy my 'lunch', but I would just buy sweets. There was no thinking about nutrition in those days.

Whatever I earned I spent. I was never a saver. Attracta was completely different. When we'd get Easter eggs as presents, weeks in advance, she would keep hers under the bed, saving them until Easter. I would open mine straight away and have it eaten – with her help. One time we got these really fancy eggs, all done up in a beautiful basket. Mine were long gone, so I started going into her room, opening up the package, eating some, and then replacing the packaging perfectly in the shape of the egg. She recalls slagging me regularly that I had eaten mine, that it was all gone, and was absolutely raging with me when she found out I had hers gone too!

In the summer I loved packing up the van and going with Dad to Connemara. They were great people out there, and it's a gorgeous drive. I still never get tired of it. We would have breakfast in Maam Cross, ham sandwiches in Recess, and Fanta and a bag of crisps in another spot.

Derek, my cousin, worked a lot with us in the fields and on the stalls, and he worked far harder than I ever did. At Christmas time we bought trees off Coillte. We had to go into the woods and take them out; very hard work. We would also make Christmas tree stands and sell them around Galway and Athenry. I'd say I was very annoying, and Derek would have thought I was very pampered, which I might have been for the time, but certainly not by today's standards.

Terence and Aidan and Damian, other cousins, were closer to Derek's age. They used to come up to see him a good bit, with my aunt Helen from Ballinrobe, and I'd always be trying to hang around with them because they were older. There would be all sorts of messing and trickery. We would often go back the road to Blythwood, an old estate that had fallen into disrepair. I was often left back there on my own, while the older cousins went cycling off and headed home without me. That's how you build up your backbone. In the summer, Attracta and Derek and I would cycle out to a swimming pool in Clarinbridge to swim. It would take about an hour and half to get there. I'd be trailing behind the others, who were much faster.

The disbanded Limerick to Galway railway line was behind our house. It's functioning again now, but back in the 1980s and early 1990s I played on it with Paul Molloy, Paul Neary, Emmet Gardiner, Darren Nally and Cathal Daly. We built huts on the line, and had loads of adventures, and used to walk on it into the town. The movie *Stand By Me* resonated with all of us because, like those boys, we were always walking up and down the railway line, building bonfires and tree huts, all the type of stuff that boys do.

I went to primary school in Athenry, and we were one of the last classes to go into the old boys' school, which had wooden desks, including inkwells, with benches built in. On the right-hand side of the school there was a patch of mud, and that's where we all played, whenever we could, and it would be drying into us all day. I was a very quiet boy at school and I was big. I was given nicknames like Burgus and Ten-Ton Betsy. By the time I got to fourth class Paul Molloy was my best mate. He was a small lad. In the mornings all the cool dudes used to pick fellas out to have a fight with, and one of the mornings they picked on Paul. Paul was getting well sorted, but I wasn't having any of it. At the age of ten I lost it for the first time and beat up a few of them. From that day on my life changed. Everybody wanted to start fighting me. I was now the lad everyone wanted to have a row with, though I was really as quiet as a mouse. But I was well able to handle myself. Then other boys realised that I could help them out, and for a while I became the defender of some of the smaller lads. It was only when I got into sports that I began hanging around with the kids who would have been fighting with me.

I also became friends with Paul Neary, whose family lived over their shop in Athenry, and we remain best friends to this day. The first time I went into their house, Catherine, his mother, thought I had gone, and she said to Paul, 'He's very chubby isn't he?' We've had a laugh about that. I don't think it bothered me too much at the time. Paul's brother, John Michael, was mentally and physically disabled. I saw John Michael every day of my life for a long time, so you would think I would have understood what it was like to have a disability, and what to expect when it happened to me, but I didn't.

There wasn't much sport in school at the time, aside from hurling, so I found it outside school. I wasn't built for GAA but as I got older I took on everything else I could: rugby, soccer, squash, basketball, tennis. I took up rugby at about the age of ten, as a way of getting out of selling cabbages on cold mornings on the square in Athenry. Two of my school friends told me they were going out to a small village called Monivea to play rugby. There was a free bus out on a Saturday morning and afterwards they gave you a free bag of chips and a can of Coke. I was sold! No other sports did that at the time. I had been playing a small bit of hurling, and all you got there was abuse. The bus left Athenry at ten o'clock, so I would put up the stall with my dad and then head off.

I have always been Fergus at home and around Athenry, but at rugby I became known as Gus, or Gussy. Then when I began playing soccer at the age of 11 or 12, I was always called Fergie. To this day three people might be talking about Gussy and Fergie and Fergus and not realise it's the same person!

I loved soccer. I was a goalkeeper and I played with Athenry, on its first underage team in years, which had been started by Johnny Delaney and Kevin Cahalan. I cycled to training, which took me past the cemetery. Dad had told me about the banshee, probably to keep a rein on me, and that the only way you would stop a banshee from catching you was to cross a crossroads. I heard the banshee everywhere (usually the wind) and I'd cycle like mad to get to the crossroads about half a mile from my house. The banshee never caught me!

Neither of my parents was into sport, and neither seemed competitive, but both my sister and I picked up the gene somewhere. Attracta and I clashed a lot because we were both so competitive. If she succeeded at something, I wanted to too. I realise now that from a young age everything I did I viewed as a competition or a challenge, even picking cabbages. I always wanted to be the quickest!

HARD WORK BRINGS REWARDS.

I was introduced to hard work at a very young age, but there was always a reward, a few pounds, a treat – or the bag of chips at the end of rugby training. We all want rewards, but we often don't want the hardship or the hard work that it takes to get them.

Social media just shows us the rewards, the end products, and that's a big problem. People just want the end result, they don't want the hardship or the sacrifices, but you need to put in the graft. I knew if I wanted the reward of even a little movement in my lower limbs I needed to work harder than I had ever worked before.

5

BIGGER AND BOLDER

As Attracta and I got older, our competitive streaks got stronger. We were both driven in everything we did. She was very good at school, but I didn't care about that. She became a champion Irish dancer, which was outside my skill set, but I threw myself into sport. If she was doing well, I wanted to do well, to be the best. I wasn't happy just playing with my club; I always wanted to go further. It was always about the next step.

Alongside the sibling rivalry, jealousy sometimes reared its head. Even when I started excelling at rugby and soccer, Dad might have come to see only one or two of my games – he was always working. Mum, however, would have been constantly going to feiseanna and competitions with Attracta. We weren't well off, so there must have been lots of sacrifices to fund costumes and travel. Dad even built her a little raised floor, with a bit of 'give' in it, to reduce her risk of injury when she was practising at home.

Attracta was a great dancer and her hard work made her an All-Ireland and World Champion. She would have performed in the first *Riverdance* except she was doing her Leaving Certificate. She wanted to get into medicine, and was very diligent, so when she didn't get enough points she repeated at Yeats College, a private school, and got a place at the Royal College of Surgeons in Dublin. At the same time she was offered a part in Michael Flatley's *Lord of the Dance*, so she deferred the place for a year. They were dancing every day and it was very hard on the body, so they had chiropractors working with them all the time. She was fascinated by what the chiropractors were doing, and how it helped them as dancers. So when she finished the tour she decided not to go to medical school but instead went to England to study and train for five years to be a chiropractor, and that's what she has been doing since.

Just before *Lord of the Dance* opened in Dublin, Attracta invited Paul Neary and myself to a preview show for family and friends. When I said we had nowhere to stay she invited us to her digs. We were 16-year-old boys, so of course we jumped at the chance to stay in a house with about a dozen female dancers. It was a lovely house on Sandymount Road looking out to sea, and we were in our element, up from Galway in Dublin on our own, surrounded by gorgeous young women.

Paul and I did most of our growing up together. His parents owned an off licence and they had a shed out the back which was beside the back lawn of Barry Kelly's parents' property. At night Paul would turn off the alarm and we'd go in and sneak out a few naggins of whatever drink we wanted to try that particular evening. We'd sit up on the top of the shed, and open the naggins. But we never liked the taste of any of them, so we'd take a little sip and then throw the full naggin over the wall into the neighbours'. We discovered later that Barry, who was a couple of years older than us, but became a great friend of mine, would find the bottles, wonder where they came from, but drink them himself!

After taking a few sips Paul and I would lie there looking at the stars and talking about rugby, and probably girls, and about what we were going to do next, because we did everything together.

Any sport he played, I played; any sport I played, he played. We were both super-competitive. There were so many times when we went to the basketball court, or down to the sports grounds to throw a rugby ball around, and we wouldn't be talking to each other on the way back at all – that's how competitive we were in everything.

When I was younger I could run through anything on a rugby pitch, but as I got older other players were learning how to tackle, so I had to improve my skills and get fitter if I wanted to keep up. Paul had fantastic pace, incredible speed, but his other skills, like catching a ball under pressure or tackling, weren't great. But because the two of us were constantly practising, constantly pitting ourselves against each other, we both improved our games. Those sessions together turned us both into better all-round players. I had the size, then I was fitter, and then I upped my skill levels, so it was just constant improvement. Looking back I can see I was setting myself challenges to improve all the time. I even started getting up before school and going for five-mile runs. I never told anyone. I just wanted to see if I could get myself even fitter.

I did alright in the Leaving Cert, but not great. I might have started tasting drink young, but because I was so committed to sport, I only had my first proper drink on the night we celebrated the results. A bunch of us went to the Meadow Court Hotel, near Athenry, for dinner and then into the nightclub. I presumed I would be able to drink like my dad or my uncle, so I knocked back a first pint of Guinness and then a second. The third time I tried to drink it down fast it didn't stay down. Within a matter of seconds the bouncers had me outside, and I spent the rest of our Leaving Cert celebrations with my head between my legs. It was a lesson learned. Like a lot of young Irish men I did a lot of drinking between the ages of 18 and 21.

I got on to an electronic engineering course in Galway, and moved into the city with friends from school. I could have stayed at home in Athenry but I wanted to move in with the lads – that's where the craic was. And I worked to pay my rent and other expenses. My parents couldn't have afforded it, though I'm sure they would have found a way if I had asked. I wasn't interested in the course, and I lasted only a month or two. I was too focused on training. I couldn't work, train and go to college.

I was happy to work at anything that would earn me a few pounds. John Cooke, a great mentor from Monivea RFC, gave me a part-time job at Cooke's corner shop on Dominick Street in Galway, which he ran with his cousin Gabriel, another gentleman. I worked alongside a woman called Catherine, who was very sound, and we got on really well. I loved chatting to customers.

It was 1998 and the first time Galway footballers had won the All-Ireland in a long, long time. I was working that night but closed up and went out afterwards with John to celebrate. The city was electric. Everyone was joining in the party. I stayed in John's house that night, as I often did, and got up to open the shop in the morning. It was quiet, and I went behind the till where there was a little shelf that you could sit on and put your feet up, to have a rest. The next thing I remember I could hear someone saying, 'Hello, hello, hello.' I had fallen asleep behind the counter and there were about five people looking over at me waiting to get served.

At this stage I was also getting paid £400 a game for Galwegians. We had about 10–12 games a year, so that was alright. It was a good week's wages back in the day. The club also got me a job as a bouncer in the GPO disco. It was an over-21s disco and I would have been around 19 at the time. I remember turning away people who were ahead of me in school and they were always getting very thick with me. 'Ah, you were in school, and you were behind us. How are you allowed to turn us away?'

It was a bit of a techno club, so there were plenty of drugs knocking about, though I was very naive. Some of the bouncers weren't that nice, but Jimmy Duffy, who played with Galwegians and the Irish under-21s, looked after me. I was a bit of an eejit. One night I phoned in sick because I wanted to go out drinking with a few lads, and the craic was too good. But where did we go at the end of the night? To the GPO! They let me in, and I had a few drinks, but they were not impressed with me. I wasn't allowed to drink there after that, but at least they allowed me to continue working.

On one of the last nights I worked at the club, I turned away two ladies, who then spat in my face. That night when I left the club I went to Supermac's to get some food, and as I was walking home a van started following me. It kept following me, and I started running. It was a good job that I was fit at the time because I had to keep running through estates trying to get away from them. After that I thought, 'This bouncer craic is just not worth it.'

I was happy living in Galway city, training, playing sport, going out and enjoying myself. It was a great life in lots of ways. The priority was always to have money for socialising. Even buying a new pair of jeans was way down the list. I wasn't the most fashionable person, so what I wore didn't bother me.

Over the next few years I would come and go between Galway and Athenry. I'd go to South Africa to play rugby for four to six months, come back and stay at home in Athenry for a while, and then move back into Galway when I had a few pounds and there was a room free. Then I went to Australia.

While all this was going on, we started building on Dad's farmland. There was a site with my name on it and I got a loan of €120,000 to build a house. I also had another site for a second house. However, I could have won a gold medal for bad timing. I built a gorgeous house, but just as I was finishing it the route of the new motorway from Ballinasloe to Galway was announced. I had hoped to make €20,000 or €30,000 profit, which was big money back in the day, but the route went within 200 metres of the house I was just after building. And the second site I had just started on was going to be on the other side of the motorway. I actually lost money on the first house. Nobody wanted it because they couldn't visualise what it would be like with the motorway so close, and I had to sell it cheap.

During 2002 and 2003 I had to complete and sell the second house, knowing I was losing money all the time. Some days it was hard to get out of bed knowing that. But I worked for two years solidly getting those houses built. I enjoyed it, and I had even planned on going into that business, developing on sites and selling on. In hindsight I was probably lucky, because if I had been successful with those sites and continued I would have been caught up when the property bubble burst in 2008 and 2009.

When my plans to be a property developer went pear-shaped, I was floundering about, twiddling my thumbs, and that's when Dad suggested I start taxiing with him.

CHALLENGE YOURSELF.

I have discovered that it is competition – external and internal – that has always spurred me on. I still view everything as a competition, a chance to beat others or challenge myself. If you challenge yourself at every small opportunity throughout the day, it will lead to huge gains. Challenge = Growth.

6

THE GAME OF RUGBY

Some of my happiest moments in rugby were wearing the red and black hoops of Monivea Rugby Football Club. Only about 86 people went to bed in the village of Monivea at the time, but they created some hugely successful teams and players.

Rugby played a huge part in making me the man I am. I ended up being a decent player, but that was largely down to my size. I was a big young lad, so you could give me the ball and I would be able to run through five or six of the opposing team. I loved the sport because everything was done as a unit. I loved the camaraderie and the team spirit, and the respect it instilled for officials and referees. You never spoke out of turn. The work ethic had started with my dad, but the work ethic of gaining fitness, and playing as a team, began at Monivea RFC.

Even as a young fella I was so impressed by the time and effort the coaches and mentors put into the club. There were great men like Padraig McGann (known as Mr Monivea around the village) and John Cooke. They didn't even have sons playing on my teams, but they brought us everywhere and we had great craic with them. And as we grew up they made sure we always had good coaches, men like Ian Calder, Neil McDonald, Richie Evans, Hohepa Dan Panapa (Jo Papa), Dan McFarland and John Muldoon.

We were the smallest country team in Ireland at the time, so we had a bit of an inferiority complex. The city teams had fancy pitches and floodlights and big changing rooms. Monivea barely had a pitch, never mind changing rooms.

Damian Browne tells a story about when he first met me. We were both about 12, and he was playing for Galwegians and I was playing for Monivea. He says I was running towards the ball and threw him a couple of punches in the kidneys on the way past. I don't remember that, but I'm sure it did happen. I was a little thug when I was younger. Our little country team was always being beaten by city teams, and because I was the biggest and strongest player on our side the city teams would target me. I took the brunt of it, but I enjoyed it, because I ended up in a lot of scraps. I'd also be jumping in when they were fighting the other lads.

You lay down your masculinity, your marker, at a very early age. You don't realise it yourself, but that's what you're doing. You're saying 'Don't mess with me!' With rugby you could do that and get away with it. It took a lot to get sent off in rugby. I was sin-binned a few times but only got red-carded once, during a match against Loughrea RFC. My boot made contact with a player's head after I kicked the ball, but the Competitions Committee later ruled that it was an accident and the card was rescinded. However, I learned quickly that a lot of behaviour wasn't deemed acceptable in other sports. I was playing my first game as goalie for Athenry Football Club's senior team. I was about 16 and had a match coming up for the Irish rugby under-18s. I had a bad infection on my leg and I never wore shin pads – back in those days you didn't have to – because they weren't comfortable on my big calves. The match wasn't long started when I made a very basic save and I slid. The fella who was following through, an older fella in his twenties, kicked me in the shin, although I was holding the ball at my chest. He kicked me right where the infection was and I was so sore and so livid that I got up and ran after him. As he was running away from me laughing I caught up with him and took the legs from under him. A rugby referee back then would have said, 'Don't be doing that, now away you go.' But this wasn't rugby. The referee sent me off. I hadn't lasted five minutes. That was my introduction to senior soccer and new rules of engagement.

I was very lucky at Monivea. I ended up playing alongside a bunch of lads who were very good. I think we were probably at our best when we got to the under-18s, when we were doing really well against bigger clubs in the provinces. I also made the Irish under-18s, and a lot of our squad got into the Connacht under-18s. That team included some of the men I still count among my best friends.

I was probably the main player on that team, but when we got to the semi-final of the cup against Westport, we lost. I blame myself a lot for the loss because I was very selfish in that game. I was playing number eight and I took on too much ball. Our coach was Noel Rabbitte, who was one of my best mates, even though he was older than me. We all loved him. He was only 20 years of age at the time, but the time and effort he put into us and our under-18 team was phenomenal. His philosophy, and it was brilliant, was: 'We don't kick away the ball, we run it from everywhere.' And we had the players to do that. We were fit, we were hungry. But in that particular game, I never kicked the ball away at all; I picked it up from the base of the scrum one too many times, and instead of passing the ball I took it on too much.

I hadn't turned 18 the year Monivea won the junior league and went into the round robin – a chance to graduate to the senior league. We had won in our province and would now play the winners of each other province to hopefully get promoted to senior status. I'd played a few small parts, subbing every now and again on the first team. Our star player was Dean Harper, a New Zealander and a pretty cocky character. Something happened leading up to the biggest match of that season, against Banbridge, and he was dropped. Ian Calder was the coach, another New Zealander, a really top-quality young coach, and he called me to say, 'Fergus, you're starting in the back row.' And I just felt 'Wow!' From the time I had started playing, I had always wanted to play for Monivea's first team, but hadn't expected it to happen so soon. This was going to be the biggest game of my life.

Unfortunately, we didn't win that game against Banbridge; we fell just short. I had a brilliant game and was named man of the match. That was a huge moment in my life, with my friends watching, and the village watching, and it made my name with the club. That under-18s team also got to the league final against Galwegians, but I wasn't around to play. I was in South Africa, and though they were favourites they lost. However, at Monivea RFC we always punched way above our weight despite the lack of silverware at underage.

I also played with Monivea under-20s, which was absolutely brilliant. That under-20s squad was another great group of players and we went to an All-Ireland series, playing against some big clubs. One game that went down in Monivea folklore was against Paul O'Connell's Young Munster in January 2000. They played us at home on a Saturday night. We had amazingly good floodlights, but no changing rooms. They had probably never seen anything like it. They had to change in old derelict changing rooms beside McGanns' pub, run down to the pitch, which is 500 metres away, play a game of rugby, and run back up again.

It was one of Monivea's many David vs Goliath moments. A lot of famous Irish internationals had gone through Young Munster, and Paul O'Connell was forging quite a reputation. He was their captain, I was ours, and we had really exceptional players: Niall O'Brien, Kevin Higgins, Cathal Divilly, Paul Neary, Phelim Cloonan, Kieran Concarr, Joe Noone, John Gavin and John Culkin. The first half didn't go our way and we were 3–24 down at half-time. They were destroying us. As we were running off the pitch into our containers – that's what we had on the sidelines – for our half-time talk, Paul O'Connell jogged over to me, said, 'Fair play for doing it for the parish', and kept going. He was telling me we were playing against the big boys. I was not a happy man going back into the rest of the team, and I got them riled up too. We refocused.

Young Munster came out thinking the game was won, but in the second half we turned it around. One big moment still stands out for me. I got the ball in the middle of the field, around the halfway mark. I think we had three players through my right and we had Paul Neary out on the wing, the fastest rugby player I've ever come across. I made a 30-metre pass, running at full tilt. It was perfect. Paul gathered the ball and ran in from about 30 or 40 metres out. When the final whistle blew we had beaten Young Munster 25–24. We were euphoric. We couldn't believe it. What a victory!

I played with far bigger teams, including the Irish under-18s, Galwegians and Connacht Juniors, but playing with Monivea gave me some of the happiest times of my life, by a country mile. It was an amazing experience to accomplish and enjoy victories like that with my mates.

* * *

I excelled at underage rugby but I actually gave it up at the age of 14 to focus on soccer, which I was enjoying more at the time. I played for Athenry, in goal for Galway Town, and made the first Connacht under-18 team.

The skill sets of both sports complemented each other. Soccer slimmed me down a bit and made me fitter, and rugby made me brave – and to be a goalkeeper you have to be brave. I always went after the ball. I was good. I even kept David Forde out of the goalie position –maybe because the selector was from my hometown – but he was the one who went on to win 24 caps for Ireland.

When I was a bit older there was a younger lad in Athenry FC called Cathal Fahey. He was very talented and at the age of 12 was being brought to trials by clubs all over England. When he was invited for a trial week with Leeds United the club organised a tour to go over with him.

It was a brilliant few days, and while we were there the organisers arranged a match against a team of prison inmates – I don't remember which one. It was strange being inside a jail, but what we couldn't get over was that they had a state-of-the-art AstroTurf pitch, at a time when no one had them. We didn't have shoes for astro so they took us into a storeroom filled with kit and told us to pick out new football boots for ourselves! The inmates on the team were the ones who had been behaving themselves, but they were fully grown adults, all tattoos and muscles, and we had a lot of younger players. We realised after about five minutes that they weren't really allowed to tackle us, or the prison guards would be down on top of them. So we started flaking into them, knowing they couldn't touch us. We ended up losing the game, but we'd had a special experience.

After a couple of years I realised I wasn't giving it my all. I had a Connacht cap and we were due to play the other provinces in a tournament in Castlebar, but I went to a twenty-first birthday party for John Michael, Paul Neary's older brother, the night before. He had a lot of disabilities and had overcome many setbacks, so it was a great celebration. I wasn't drinking but I stayed out until about 5 a.m., which I shouldn't have done. Paul had to drive me to Castlebar the next morning for the matches, and I was exhausted. You need full concentration and focus in goals.

I had already, at about the age of 16, been drawn back to rugby, and the team unit of rugby started appealing to me more and more. While soccer was all built on hatred for the other team, rugby was built on respect. You might be killing each other on the pitch but the minute that was done it was all about respect. The game also seemed to involve more camaraderie and craic; and I have always liked a bit of craic, no matter how serious I am about my sport.

I made the Connacht under-18s team a couple of years in a row, then I was brought forward for the Ireland under-18s trials, and I made that squad in 1998. I was so thrilled that I put even more of an effort into my fitness and training.

I was anxious to progress, but it didn't go as I had hoped. Academy contracts are given to young players to put them on the road to being professional players. At the time one might include a small payment, accommodation and a training programme for the year. I had just done my Leaving Cert and all the Connacht players who had made the Irish squads got their academy contracts, and so did others who didn't make the Irish squad. But I didn't get offered anything.

At that time our fantastic coach in Monivea, Ian Calder, had taught me a lot, and he'd given me lots of one-on-one sessions to get me fitter and better. When he heard that I hadn't received a contract he asked me if I wanted to go to South Africa for the summer. He had played and coached there himself. Two other Monivea lads, Noel Rabbitte and Michael Cannon (who we called Flash) were already signed up to go down on an exchange programme to train and play and improve. I had been playing with Flash and Noel on the Monivea senior squad since I was 16, and Noel coached our under-18 team, which had done so well. South Africa were world champions at the time, and Ian told me I could make a name for myself on the field. I couldn't turn down the chance, and less than two weeks later I was gone.

The furthest from home I'd been was London, once for a Connacht underage weekend away and once with my parents. Now I was heading to South Africa. To say we were all naive was an understatement. We arrived into Heathrow, I think it was Terminal 1, and our connecting flight to Johannesburg was from Terminal 3. So instead of taking the shuttle bus we decided we had loads of time and we would walk – surely it couldn't be that far? Two hours later we were still walking through corridors following signs for Terminal 3.

The flight was half empty, so we had whole rows of seats to ourselves. South Africa wasn't really on the tourist map at that time. During the middle of the night, the plane was in cruise mode and it was very quiet. Flash woke up all of a sudden, looked around with a startled face and said, 'Have we stopped?' And Noel said, 'Yeah, we've stopped to refuel.' Flash just turned around, put his head down and went back to sleep.

When we arrived into Johannesburg, we had to wait for a connecting flight to a place called Richards Bay, which is on the east coast, close to Durban. We walked outside the terminal building to get some air, and the heat just hit us. We had never experienced anything even remotely like that heat or humidity. The three pasty white Irish lads were struggling so much with the heat and humidity that we had to lie down on the tarmacadam.

It was a small plane down to Richards Bay, where we were picked up by Empangeni RFC club president Chris Evans, an absolute gentleman. We stayed in a section of a boarding school; we had our own wing but we ate in the same hall as the students. And that was very entertaining. The club, which was in Natal, about two hours north of Durban, had a beautiful setup. To our amazement it even had its own stand, though this was a town of only about 100,000 people with two shopping centres.

It was an instant culture shock. In Ireland at that time, not to mind rural Galway, you rarely saw someone who wasn't white. There was only one black person in our town at the time, and now we were the minority. But though the vast majority of locals were black, we were in the heart of Afrikaans country, so very few of them played rugby. I would estimate only 5 per cent of the whole training squad weren't white. I also couldn't get over how developed and sophisticated South Africa was at that time, compared to Ireland, in terms of infrastructure and lifestyle, or how well off so many of the white people were.

The heat was horrendous and we learned quickly to down gallons of water to keep hydrated. We also had to pick up on other local club customs. We weren't long there when I was playing in the back row in a match with the third team, and the humidity and heat was extremely high. At half-time everyone headed back into the dressing room. There was a huge barrel of water there and as the players came in they ducked their big sweaty heads in it to cool down. But I hadn't seen them doing that, and I ran in, bent down, and took a big slug of water out of it. I got some slagging over that!

We gradually got used to the heat while training and pushing ourselves really hard. I had never trained in a gym, but it was all part of how the team prepared, so we started learning how to work out and got our fitness levels up. I enjoyed it so much that I even did extra training. I just wanted to get better – I'd do anything to improve. I started introducing my own exercises, like hopping up steps on one leg to strengthen my core and improve my speed and agility.

In Natal I was doing well, and the older lads were really looking out for me, but it was out there I realised what a home bird I am, and I struggled at times. So I wasn't too disappointed when I suffered a bad shoulder injury, damage to my rotary cuff, which ended my stay. I had to come home.

To progress my career I joined Galwegians, Galway's Senior Club – and home to my idol Eric Elwood. I could still represent Monivea juniors under dual status. If your club was a junior club, you could always go up to senior. But you couldn't go from a senior club down into a junior club. One weekend I played with the Monivea under-20s on Friday night, Galwegians seniors on Saturday, and Monivea juniors on Sunday. It was pure daft, but I loved it.

I also made the Connacht under-20s squad. Unfortunately, in a match against Ulster I dislocated and damged my left ankle. They wouldn't bring me to hospital in the North so I travelled home on the bus floor in agony. I didn't do my rehab well. Maybe this was the first sign of giving up on myself?

I went back to South Africa the following year, and the year after that, each time to a different club for about three to four months. It was a brilliant experience, which gave me a very different outlook on life.

My final trip to South Africa was when Galwegians sent me over for the pre-season with Damo Browne to train, to get our heads down. I had lived with Jason Powell, a South African, the previous year. His twenty-first birthday was actually the same day as mine, and we were invited to his home place, about a nine-hour drive away up towards Kruger Park, for the party. The dress code was black and white with a splash of colour, and the South African lads told us that was code for fancy dress. So four Monivea lads – myself, Joe Noone, Phelim Cloonan and John Gavin headed off. After the long trip we had planned to cool off in Jason's pool with a few beers, until we discovered his pet pythons liked to cool off there too – and I hate snakes!

The next day when people began to arrive for the party, we realised 'a splash of colour' meant a colourful tie or scarf, but I turned 21 dressed in a short skirt, boots and a blonde wig with pigtails – a 100kg, six foot one Britney Spears.

Back home I wasn't happy with my progression. At Galwegians I would have been subbing behind Connacht seniors or Irish internationals, but because I was young and fit and eager, I believed I should have been starting. Nobody said to me, 'Hold on, Fergus, you're only twenty-one. Relax.'

I never got an academy contract. I was playing the rugby of my life, and possibly close to getting one, when I received an invitation to play with Sydney University. Kevin Dinneen (Dino), another great coach, told me, 'Don't go. You're making a bad decision.' But I was sick of hearing that my time would come. I fucked off to Australia. But I never played a game. I got injured again.

VALUE THE VOLUNTEERS.

People look up to soccer players and athletes and celebrities on social media, and of course some of them can be inspirational, but it is the local sports coaches and volunteers who are more inspirational to me, who are the real heroes. Volunteers give their time freely for the benefit of their communities, for their local teams, for other people's children, and they do it without looking for thanks or reward, or applause. Anyone who volunteers should be valued. Ireland wouldn't exist without volunteers.

7

THE THRILL OF THE TACKLE

As I got older I discovered how much I enjoyed the physicality of rugby. Some players have ball skills, some players have speed, some players can read the game better. But other players have strength, and that was my main asset. And because of soccer, and my own training, I was very fit for my size.

If you are competitive you use whatever you possess to get ahead. If I had had more skills, would I have evolved into a less aggressive player? Perhaps. But I was a big strong man and not much hurt me, so I used whatever strength I had to win. Some people don't have that in them, but winning is always my ultimate goal, in pretty much everything. I don't mean to sound horrible, but that's the reality. When it comes to challenges and competition I don't like to lose. I lose a lot, but it doesn't mean I like it.

I spent a lot of time in hospital. Even when I was younger there was a running joke around Monivea that I had been in every hospital in Connacht, with different injuries and concussions. The concussions got to such a state that one day I was in Athlone at a Connacht under-18s training session in Buccaneers, and I hit a tackle bag and just fell down. The next thing I remember I was back in Galway at the A&E. I didn't remember the training session. I didn't remember leaving the training ground. I didn't remember the car journey down to Galway.

I played a lot of indoor soccer with my mates, and even though

I'd had a concussion I'd still play. One Wednesday night I was running up the wing of the indoor gym when a guy tackled me from behind and took my legs out, and I hit my head full whack off the solid concrete wall. I was completely out of it – again. That Saturday there was an Ireland under-18s rugby trial in Mullingar, and I couldn't say anything to the Irish team about it, but I was in a bad way. I shouldn't have played, but I did. We didn't really understand about concussions back in those days, and I just kept how bad I was a secret. No surprise that I didn't play well.

Galwegians held a tournament called the Blakes 10s, where teams from around Ireland came and played 10-a-sides. I wasn't on the Galwegians team, but Monivea had a team in the competition, and both sides had a lot of extra players left over, so we joined together and made another team. We ended up actually winning the tournament, which was brilliant, because there were some really great teams involved. During that tournament I got a knee to the face and split my lip open. I was out of it. Damo escorted me into the dressing room, to let me recover, and left me alone, thinking I was well enough to get changed. But there was a women's tournament going on at the same time and apparently I wandered buck naked into the showers, where there was a group of women showering. Someone heard their screaming and Damo had to come in and get me out, sit me down and mind me. I was totally out of it. When my sister came to collect me hours later I was up on the stage at the post-tournament dinner getting my winner's medal, with a huge cut from my nose to my lip, and obviously looking the worse for wear. I still wasn't sure where I was or what was going on. She took me to hospital, where they realised I was concussed and needed to be stitched up between my nose and my upper lip.

I don't remember being taken off too often, but I did find a report of a Galwegians vs Blackrock match in the *City Tribune* from March 2004, which said the referee had 'bizarrely ruled Fergus Farrell unfit to continue, despite the Monivea prop looking utterly bemused by the decision and protesting his fitness from the sideline'. That sounds about right! But I was actually okay on that occasion. The captain had asked me to stay down for longer to give the team a breather. It was my second 'injury' and the referee put me off and said I had to be replaced. However, back in the day head injuries usually weren't seen as a concern at all. You didn't complain, you moved on. In hindsight that was unfortunate, because I probably am still suffering the after-effects of all those knocks.

Looking back, though, the pros of playing rugby outweighed the cons and I'd never change a minute of it. I enjoyed my youth. I got to Australia. I got to South Africa. I played some very good rugby with Monivea, Galwegians and the Connacht juniors. By the time I was heading into my late twenties I had the bus company and I'd drive the bus for the team, play a game for them, and bring them home. Connacht juniors is a good level down, and I didn't really have to train that hard, to bust a gut. I was trying to build my business, so rugby was playing second fiddle. I finally gave it up when I realised I just hadn't the commitment to it any more. You need full commitment.

I still have a lot of time and respect for the rugby community. In June 2023 I was really honoured to be awarded the Unsung Hero Award at the Connacht Rugby Awards dinner. It was a great night, and I was so grateful to everyone in the Connacht rugby community, especially Joe Gorman, who nominated me.

My position in rugby evolved over the years. As a massive heavy young lad I was in the front row, a loosehead or tighthead prop. But as I started getting fitter, between the ages of 16 and 18, I moved into the back row. I played either 8 or 6, which I really enjoyed, because you get your hands on the ball a whole lot more. I was also alternated between there and the front row. When I went to Galwegians I moved back into the front row. I was a loosehead but they trained me up as a tighthead. I was way too light for a tighthead at that stage. I was 16 stone, and you need to be at least 17½ or 18 stone, and a few years older. I wasn't aware of that at the time, but I would have done anything to try and make that first team.

There's a big difference between being a loosehead and a tighthead in terms of scrummaging, but the beauty of being a tighthead is you are the anchor of the team. If you can hold up your scrum, you give your team a massive advantage, because you can play front foot rugby. So I used to love that, especially as I got older. At the time I really wanted to be in the back row. I was a very agile, fit tighthead prop, but I was too light, and that really went against me. Other props I would have been up against were 19 and 20 stone, so I took a lot of battering.

When I was younger I scored tries for fun, but as I got older and bigger and slower I wasn't scoring as much. However, it wasn't the tries that meant the most to me. It was the hits and the tackles, dominating other guys, that was the fun for me, and you could do that as a tighthead. I loved the confrontation and the aggression, and I could do that in spades in the front row, because I was always engaging in the scrum. I'd be a metre back from the opposition, and I'd fire myself into it and try to engage them and beat them over the ground.

On a team everybody's work has value, but this is especially true in rugby. A rugby team is a very, very powerful unit, but you're only as good as the guy beside you. An individual can't excel without the team. When I played rugby it was the team I thought about. The harder I worked, the fitter I was, the better the team would do.

Teamwork remained important to me in business, and in life. We all hear about the culture in a business, but ultimately it's all about relationships – between the people within the business and the people using that business. Relationships are the key to every team, especially on the rugby field. There is a scrum-half out-half relationship. There is a front row relationship. If you ever look at a rugby team the front rowers will always hang out together, because they have the same mindset. The wingers and full backs, and maybe centres, will hang out together because they've got the same mindset. The numbers 9 and 10 – the brains behind the team – will hang out together. A team will all go out together, but if you're in a pub you'll probably see all the props taking over a corner.

Most of my rugby mates, Joe Noone, Kevin Ward, Alex Dolan, Damo Browne and Noel Rabbitte were forwards. We are big mullackers getting our heads stuck into everything. That's not a criticism, that's our mindset; we have the same type of personality. Of course I had friends from outside the props and the front rows and back row. Paul Neary is a winger, but on a night out Paul would probably be off talking to his mates. The wingers and fullbacks and centres are the fancy lads. They dress up properly for a night out, and fuss about their hair – and would be hopeful that they might get lucky. Whereas us props are big fellas who just throw on our clothes and are more interested in the pints and the craic.

The drinking culture was a big part of playing rugby then, and it was even more extreme in South Africa. They'd be dancing up on the top of bars wearing just their jocks. Unlike GAA players, who didn't know their playing schedule, we knew what weekends we were off, and we could let off steam.

Back in Galway, one day before Christmas, we went down to Taaffes pub in the early afternoon after being out the night before. We had no plans to stay drinking. But Alex Dolan disappeared and came back with a load of Santa suits that he had bought in the discount store. So we all dressed up – this was a time before people started dressing up around Christmas – and just sat in Taaffes having a few pints, and because we were big guys we all looked the part. The word spread around town and people were sending their kids in to have a look at these 12 Santas. We went on to another pub and another pub, and more people kept joining us. That's where the idea of the Latin Cross came from. There are 21 pubs in the streets of Galway's Latin Quarter that make a cross, and someone started up this idea of a pint in every pub. I've never completed it. I've only come close to it a few times, but I think Damo and Noel made it.

Despite what it might seem I'm not a big drinker, though despair did occasionally drive me to drink more than normal after my accident. I might go weeks, even months, without a drink. I rarely drank when I was in business, and I never keep it in the house. However, when I do drink it will be more than a few pints, a bit of a binge, just like it was when I was playing rugby.

If I get together with the lads we still have great craic, just silliness, a lot of slagging. We always wanted to succeed. We took playing and training seriously, but we valued the social side too. The game has become much more serious now, but I think you have to enjoy yourself as well.

Looking back over my life, I began to wonder if I had been bigger with my ambitions and goals, if I had always seen every day as a day to improve, could I have gone further in rugby, could I have pushed myself more? I had visualised myself in the Irish under-18s shirt, but if I had just seen that as a stepping stone, could I have achieved more? But would I have been happy if I had made it as a professional player? I'm not sure. I played rugby first and foremost for the craic, the camaraderie. That's why I loved my final playing days with Monivea. Professional rugby might not have been so enjoyable. Maybe, if I had been more focused at that time, I could have gone further, but I was loving the training, the playing, and the social life around it. The years between 16 to 23 were probably the happiest in my life, a time when I was playing a lot of sport and having a lot of fun.

WE ALL NEED A TEAM.

None of us can excel without the team around us, to support us. Everybody's work has value, but the harder you work, the better your team will do. Good relationships are the key to any good team, in sport, in business, in families.

8

MAKING A FAMILY

It was March 2003. I was about to leave for Australia and on a night out with the rugby lads when I first met Mandy in Central Park, a famous Galway nightclub that kickstarted a lot of local marriages. One of my mates was trying to chat her up, but she was having none of it. But later in the night I went over and started talking to her and we clicked.

We met up a couple of times before I left for Australia and got on really well. She was a nurse, and just back from a tour of South Africa, which I knew well, and we had loads to talk about. We were both chatty.

Then I flew off to Australia, where I was meant to be for at least a year. We continued texting and talking occasionally – back in those days there was no WhatsApp – and we got on really well. But then I got injured and came home after about three months. I had been a total idiot over there. I didn't even leave Sydney, I just spent all my money drinking and partying, but through it all I was keeping in touch with Mandy.

The first thing I did when I got back was meet up with her, and we took it from there. She really accepted me as I was, a fella trying to play a bit of rugby who was working with his dad driving a taxi and a minibus.

One of the first times we went out I was bringing her out to Athenry, and I collected her in one of the minibuses. Brendan Lynskey's bar – The Fields – was changing hands, so there was free drink for the regulars, and I was one of those regulars. We were going out to meet Barry Kelly, who I had become great friends with, but on the way the bus broke down and we didn't even get to the pub.

I just fell in love with her. She is an absolutely fantastic woman. We loved travelling together, and we got on so well. In 2005 we took our holidays for the Lions Tour. At this stage I had been seeing her for two years and I knew she was the one for me. I had a ring made by a jeweller up in Dublin and I stuck the ring in my bag. We went to New Zealand, and Brisbane, but my plan was to propose to her in Sydney, in Darling Harbour, where we were staying. She loved boats, and I was going to hire a little boat and propose to her in the harbour. But on the day I had planned to do that we both went off separately to meet friends who were living in Sydney. We both ended up getting drunk and losing contact, so she was upset and annoyed when we finally did meet up. It wasn't the right time! So the next morning I just went down on my knee in the apartment and proposed.

A friend, Johnny Melia, heard we had got engaged, and he and his girlfriend invited us out for dinner to a very fancy restaurant in The Rocks, a suburb of Sydney.

Mandy and I loved Rome when we visited it together, and decided we would get married there. However, when we returned to plan the ceremony we realised it would be too hot in summer for us temperate Irish! So we were married in July 2007 at the Lady Gregory Hotel in Galway. Paul Neary was my best man, Derek Carroll and Joe Noone were my groomsmen, and I asked Barry Kelly to drive the wedding car for us, an old Rolls-Royce that Dad had bought. It was a great day out, and we went off on our honeymoon to British Columbia and Alberta, a road trip up into the mountains, Calgary, Jasper, Banff, Whistler. One morning, about a week in, Attracta called to tell me that Barry had been killed in a car accident.

I was devastated. He was a few years older than me, but I had played rugby with him, and had got to know him well when I was in South Africa for the second time with Johnny Melia, and he had come over for a holiday. We started looking at how we could get home. We were a six-hour drive from the nearest airport. When we were told the funeral arrangements, we realised that we mightn't make it back in time for the funeral even if we left straight away. Barry was the life and soul of Athenry, a loveable rogue, and such a good man. I still miss him. He was the second friend to die; Michael 'Flash' Cannon, who I had been in South Africa with in 1998, was killed in 2001. He was hit by a truck one foggy morning on the way home from a wedding. It was another great loss to the Athenry community. As a 14 year old I had played with both of them on a very successful Monivea RFC U18s cup-winning team. They were good men, taken too young.

* * *

Aimee was born in 2011, Bradley in 2013 and Felim in 2018. And although Mandy and I had chosen not to get married in Rome, we did return to my favourite city on a stopover during a Mediterranean cruise. I also got to go back there under different circumstances. A few years before the accident I took my dad to Rome as my mum doesn't like travelling. On our last day we went to go to the Vatican Museums but they were closed because it was All Saints' Day. So we were in St Peter's Basilica, taking in the grandeur, when we noticed a group of cardinals going up the middle and behind the main altar. We walked over to where there was a barricade open and saw that Pope Francis was in the procession. We decided to follow the entourage and we slipped in behind it, seconds before the barricade was closed. We followed the procession behind the altar to where the pope was saying mass in Latin. There were no chairs left, so we stood at the back, and we stayed there even when chairs became free after communion. When mass was over the Swiss Guards created a guard of honour, a cordon, alongside the aisles so the pope could leave. We were right up at the edge of the barricade, but as the procession and the pope came towards us my dad stood back and let in a family with young children take his place at the front. Pope Francis saw what he had done and came over and put his hand on Dad's shoulder, before walking on. That was a special moment. I want to have moments like that with my own children.

I have already taken Bradley to Rome and he was a trooper. He walked everywhere and he never complained once, even with only a few hours' sleep! I thought he'd love the Colosseum, but he loved the Vatican Museums even more. He thought they were so impressive.

I love bringing the my children on holidays, and I want them to enjoy the experience of travelling, and going to new places, like I do. We were in Turkey together recently. I love seeing their reaction to new places.

I want to make sure that they are healthy, though I'm probably not proactive enough in making sure they don't watch too much TV. I've brought them to Croke Park. I've brought them to the

Aviva Stadium. Even during lockdown I was bringing them out to different beaches, to climb Diamond Hill, to get them out and about, and to find what they enjoy, what they like.

I want them all to find sports that they enjoy. The boys have no interest in playing rugby; they play soccer. Aimee is a great rugby player – fast and strong – but she's also a great soccer player too, and that's the sport she has chosen. We are both Liverpool fans and I took her to see the Liverpool vs Bayer Leverkusen Champions League match in November 2024.

Felim is still too young to appreciate travel, but because he loves figuring out how things work and all kinds of vehicles, I bought him a quad bike for his birthday, and he's told me 'it was the best present ever'.

I have learned that the shared experiences are what matters, but I have only learned that since my accident, as I rebuilt my relationships with my children.

Mandy and I are divorced now. I didn't fight about anything. She has the house and everything else she wanted. I didn't want any more conflict. I just wanted to be with my kids, and I was heartbroken when I didn't get to see them. They are now my everything because of all I put them through, including the trauma of my accident, the separation and the aftermath. I'm happy to say that Mandy and I now have a good relationship as co-parents and I still treasure all the time we had together, including those 12 years of marriage.

TAKE EVERY CHANCE TO TRAVEL.

It's so important to take every opportunity to see new places that comes our way. If you can get the chance to explore this world, take it. Discovering new places and people, at home and abroad, is never a waste of time. My love for travel is something I want to pass on to my children. I believe travel broadens the mind and our horizons. It helps us understand the world a whole lot better, and to realise how lucky we have it in this country.

Appreciate how lucky we are to be able to travel, to get around, when so many people cannot. Never underestimate the gift of good mobility and health, because they can be taken away from you in a second. When you have your mobility, when you have your health, look after yourself, both physically and mentally, and get out into the world. Climb a mountain, run a 10k, swim in the sea. There's so many other people who wish they could.

9

11 G 563

My dad gave up the fruit and veg growing business in the late 1990s because there was just no money in it any more, but he still had a mortgage. So he went into the taxi business. He always worked hard – both my parents did – and I helped him out on the busy nights.

When I was around 23 rugby had gone past me, and my dad could see I was turning into a good-for-nothing. So he said, 'Why don't you get a licence and come drive with me?' He bought a small LDV bus to do nightclub runs, and then a Mercedes 709 bus, and I drove them. We worked together for about two or three years, but we were always at each other. We're not good business partners. So we made a decision that I would take over the bus side of things.

I grew the business nicely, and I set up a Galway–Athenry service route in March 2008, a commuter bus, in opposition to Bus Éireann. We also had five Bus Éireann school runs at the time, and I had been warned by another operator to watch out if I went up against them on any route. All our routes were put out for tender again, and we got none of them, even the one I put in a ridiculously low bid on, below running costs, just to see what would happen.

So I had five buses with nothing to do, but I had built up my private business quite well, and the service runs were finally picking up; you always lose money on them at first while you build up the clientele and the customers.

Then the recession hit. But we were lucky because we weren't relying on only one source of customers. We had clubs and schools, the service runs and the nightclub runs, all of which were different avenues of income. It was difficult, but I wasn't worried. Because there was no tour work going on, the whole market was flooded with top-end coaches, and it was a race to the bottom in terms of rates between many of the other bus companies. But I sat back and didn't join that race. I started thinking about what wasn't in the bus industry, what niche I could find to get us through. It was time to think outside the box.

I started looking through magazines and online at vehicles, and the first thing that caught my attention was a double-decker coach in the UK which was as cheap as chips because the market was collapsing over there as well. I got that and did it up and used the best drivers to drive it.

Then I began looking at all the team coaches in England, the premium ones with kitchens and tables, set up like a train, and realised there was none of those here. So I travelled over and bought one. It had been sitting idle for eight or nine months, and I got it cheap. Buying a new one of those coaches would have cost €400,000, but I bought it for €15,000, and even though it was over ten years old that was great value at the time. The coach broke down a few times on the way home, but when we gave it a full service it never missed a beat. To this day, it was the nicest vehicle I ever had. We had a contract with Connacht Rugby, so we branded up the whole bus, and everyone loved it. It really added to the atmosphere on match days. Other rugby clubs also wanted to use it, and then lads wanted to go on weekends away and stags in the Connacht coach!

I bought a second coach, and branded it up for Mervue United, who had got into the FAI league, and then a third one. I was good at looking outside the box and seeing what wasn't there, and that saved that business during the crash. And I came out of it in a brilliant state. When everyone else was on their knees, Farrell Travel was expanding.

In 2011 I bought my first brand new bus when nobody could buy anything. I'll never forget it. It was a maroon BMC Charisma, 35-seater, 11 G 563. It was a beautiful machine, automatic gearbox, the whole lot, everything was just lovely. I was so excited about going to buy my first new bus, I was like a kid at Christmas. I was picking it up in the UK, and I missed my flight from Knock for some reason, but I had to get there because I had the ferry booked for the next day to drive it back. I was picking it up near Manchester, so I managed to get a flight into Liverpool from Shannon. I didn't get into Liverpool until 11 o'clock at night, and I had a basic hotel room booked, but when I got there they had given it away because I was so late.

I could feel the excitement about my new bus draining from me. I was exhausted. But then the woman at reception told me to hold on, and a few minutes later she said they were upgrading me to a suite, if that was alright! They had two penthouse suites, one called the Kop, after the stand in the Liverpool ground, and the other called the Toffees, for Everton. And they gave me the Kop. What a room! Though it was a bit of a waste for someone on their own and just spending a few hours there. There was a Jacuzzi in the sitting room area. There was a kitchen. There was a four-poster bed. There was a gym. And they told me that Robbie

Keane, who had just left Liverpool, had stayed there. What a treat for a Liverpool fan!

I picked up the bus and it was such a joy driving home. I got it registered and put it on the service run because it had better fuel efficiency, more reliability. The first guy I gave the bus to was Johnny Brennan, a great friend who started driving for me during the recession. He was a really good driver, but on its very first trip he caught the side of it as he was pulling into his own house. It had been christened!

That was my first big bus, and then I bought a new one from Scania, which cost about €265,000. Buying that was a fantastic experience because they flew me over to San Sebastian, a beautiful town, and put me up in the fabulous five-star Santa Maria Hotel, entertained me, and brought me on a factory visit.

I could do it all because I had many different layers of businesses, from clubs to schools. I never refused work. And now I had the vehicles to get the best-paid work. We got contracts for tours because we had the newer vehicles. That's how I ended up growing.

Citylink then brought me in to do relief work, and then they asked me to tender for the Limerick run, which I did. I won the contract, with Vincent Brennan as my right-hand man helping me run the business. I also really wanted to get into the tour business, but I wanted to get in at the high end. So I brought in a transport manager who had experience, and he got me in the door with Trafalgar Tours, first on an ad hoc basis. The next season we secured a contract to do tours with them in Ireland and Europe, so we went to the bank and financed six additional coaches for it, on top of the 15 tour coaches we already had.

The vast majority of our business was now with two companies, Citylink and Trafalgar, and that's when I started making mistakes.

***

We got our six new coaches for our Trafalgar Tours work at the end of March 2016. They looked incredible all lined up; even officials from the banks who had lent us the money were taking pictures. Because of the contract I had expected that the wheels of all six buses should be turning by mid-April, but come mid-May, I still only had three or four coaches out on the road. The rest were still sitting there, not making money.

That's when the first pinch came, where the first cashflow problems began. We'd had to put down over €160,000 in deposits for those coaches, and because the tour business was a month-to-month invoice, our first big payment from Trafalgar didn't come until July. It all began to have a knock-on effect.

During that time we missed payments for our Citylink drivers in Limerick. Two weeks in a row our wages were late, and even though that was sorted, people were annoyed, and I fully understand why they would be. So when one of the drivers started saying that drivers on other Citylink routes were being paid more per hour – which they weren't – our drivers became more disgruntled.

In June 2017 we got wind that another operator was coming in to take over our routes in Limerick, and some of our drivers were jumping ship. This had been going on for weeks behind our back, and the Citylink contract was taken away from us overnight, losing us cashflow of about €25,000 per week.

We won a judgment against Citylink in arbitration, but they just refused to pay the €132,000 and costs we were awarded by the adjudicator. They were a big multinational and they knew I couldn't afford to take them to the High Court. I received an unexpected call from one of their executives after the arbitration, who more or less told me that they would use all their financial resources to take me on. I was so angry after that call I was shaking.

Losing that contract was the catalyst for everything that followed. On the same day we got wind that another company was taking over our routes, I had been finalising a deal with Mercedes-Benz. We would be selling, maintaining, offering 24-hour assistance and repairing air conditioners for the Mercedes-Benz bus and coach industry in the west of Ireland. It was huge. And I had worked my ass off for it.

We had secured a unit up in Athlone for this new business, National Coach Maintenance Services (NCMS), and we were all very excited. I felt that this was the culmination of years of hard work, and that it would secure our financial future. I had finance for a 24-hour recovery van, and I had hired someone who knew all the Mercedes products and warranties. We were building up a really great team, including my cousin Derek. We had all the right ingredients.

But while the bus company was struggling to keep up with payments, I still had to find money to keep setting up NCMS. There were substantial costs and I knew I could expect to be losing money for the first two years. The pressures began to stack up. We had taken an additional €1 million in finance to get four new coaches just four months previously. We asked the bank to take the pressure off by putting a pause on payments, but we spent months dealing with them, sending figures and filling forms, before they agreed to do that.

There were other layers of stress. We had a chauffeur business up in Dublin to complement the bus business and I was constantly getting calls from the airport during the night and in the early hours of the morning. The American flights would be coming at four or five o'clock in the morning and someone wouldn't have organised the cars correctly.

For NCMS we had hired a German mechanic called Sylvio Rose, who had a lot of Mercedes-Benz experience, even before the deal had been signed off on. We couldn't figure out why he kept cancelling going on a refresher course to England to keep up his qualification, but then we discovered that he had been charged with child pornography offences and his passport had been taken by the gardaí. He hadn't been convicted at that stage, and we were advised we had to keep him working there for another two months to make sure we went through the proper processes. It was very hard working alongside that man, but we eventually got rid of him. In 2018 he pleaded guilty to knowingly distributing child pornography and was named in news reports. He was jailed for five years.

Then our second mechanic injured himself, so now we had none.

In the middle of all this there were domestic pressures. We owned a house in Athenry, but I had designed our dream house for a site on my dad's land. However, planning permission was running out and we had to make a decision. I had been left a house by my aunt Mary Ann, out of the blue. It was almost derelict, so we had to decide whether to do up her farmhouse and sell the site with the planning permission or sell the farmhouse. We decided to build. I sold Mary Ann's farmhouse, and we also sold up our family home, and moved into my grandmother's old house – beside my parents – while we built our own. I had to borrow about €80,000 of the money from the sales to put into the business, just to keep things going.

I was thinking about the problems and the pressures night and day. Some stuff I just buried, because there were so many problems I couldn't deal with all of them: the threat of vehicles being taken by finance companies; worries about drivers breaking down or crashing. I was working seven days a week, a minimum of 12 hours and up to 18 hours a day. I was even getting emails and texts from irate and upset employees telling me I was destroying the business. A lot of people stuck with me, but others went, and I can't blame them. They could see it was all beginning to crumble.

I was trying to fight two battles. Both companies were losing money hand over fist. Everything was imploding. Finally, I had to make a decision. I stood back and decided that the company that would cost the least to fold was NCMS. The bus business was so highly leveraged that if I had closed it down I would have owed millions. I felt terrible because of the people I had hired for NCMS, but I couldn't sustain it any more. It was a devastating decision. Mercedes were fantastic about it, but the pressures kept coming. We had also lost our contract with a ski company, under which we would pick up school parties in England and take them to ski in northern Italy, in Aosta, near Turin. I loved doing that, driving through the Mont Blanc tunnel, through the Alps.

I got into buses because I love driving. However, when you start getting bigger, you have to drive less and manage more. I was good at building a team, putting good people around me – I had learned that in rugby. But when it came to the actual management of the business, I probably failed. I let it become too top-heavy – highly leveraged with loads of finance – because I wanted the big contracts. That's why it collapsed when that Citylink contract was taken away from us. I had 35 coaches on the road and every one was financed. If I hadn't been so top-heavy, I might have been able to survive.

Being top-heavy also becomes a trap. I got into a position where I was so highly leveraged that I had to start taking on extra work to keep the vehicles paid for, and then I had to start taking on extra employees. Ultimately, the quality of my product was getting lower and lower as I had to be less particular about the people I was taking on. I just needed to keep the vehicles moving. Vehicles in the yard cost too much money, so I was taking on lower-paid work to fill the gaps, but then I was also taking on employees who would cost me more money because they would damage the vehicles. So it was a double whammy. My warning to anybody going big would be to watch that pitfall: taking on work you don't need to take on, and taking on employees that are going to cost you.

I also wasn't a great delegator. Even though I always had good lads, I would jump in and pick up the slack or take on a run or a problem when something went wrong. I'd be the one to get up from dinner or leave a Sunday with my family to shoot off and sort something. I felt it was all on me. I'd be the one to get on a flight and take over a bus or fill in when a tour driver went sick. And in the meantime everything else I should have been doing was piling up. I suppose I wanted to control everything.

So there was over a year of constant fire-fighting, and it was all coming through me. I wouldn't let it out. I felt they were all my problems, my headaches. When I look back at it I don't know how I survived it, but to me it was just life. I just got on with it. Keeping the head down, absorbing the stress was ingrained in me. That's what my dad did. You get up and you get on with things, and you just keep fighting; you don't let stress get to you. Actually I didn't even believe in the word because to be stressed, you have to have time to think that you're stressed, and I didn't have time. I was going from one problem to the next, to the next to the next, to the next …

I was able to manage everything when things were going well, but it was when one thing came after another after another that I reached the tipping point. Mandy could see when I got home that I was in a bad place, but I'd never, ever tell her the depth of what was going on because I just couldn't. Maybe that's a man thing? I couldn't share what was going on, and it got to the point where there was just too much to share. If I had started telling her, or anyone, I'd have still been talking days later. Even in hindsight, I don't even know if I would have opened up to her or asked her to share that load. It was too much. Some of that was pride.

The calls and the texts were a constant barrage. Being on the phone constantly dealing with business was the norm, putting out fires, and trying to keep things going. And then there were the calls and messages looking for money, and there was no way I was showing those to her, putting pressure on her, but I still had to deal with it.

With NCMS gone I started concentrating on the bus business again, trying to get everything back on track. I just worked and worked. I had become obese, but didn't realise it. I couldn't even walk up the stairs without losing breath. Coming into October 2018, coming into the winter, I was seeing the light ahead for the first time. I believed that we were going to survive. But then 26 October came, and I lifted that bench, and it all came crashing down again.

CHANGE YOUR PERCEPTION OF SUCCESS.

Think about how you perceive success. We're conditioned to look at what we don't have – the big house, expensive car and fancy holidays. Chances are the person with all those – like I had – are the ones in crippling debt.

Real success is about having a life where you are not smothered by debt, where you are not constantly rushing, where you have time for yourself, time for others, and time to pause and enjoy the moment.

10

EARLY DAYS AT THE NRH

I didn't know what to expect at the National Rehabilitation Hospital, but it was a total shock in so many ways. The old hospital was still in use, and it was a horrible-looking building. Inside it was like an old school or convent, with windows so high that you couldn't even look out. I was taken upstairs to a shabby 16-bed ward. There was barely room for a wheelchair to fit in beside the bed, and if I put out my hand I could have touched the patient in the bed beside me. I was taken aback to realise that it was a mixed ward; there was a man on one side of me and a woman on the other. The 16 of us shared two toilets.

I arrived flat on my back, paralysed from the waist down, but I was stunned when I saw the condition of some of the other patients. I quickly realised how lucky I was. I was in a bad way, but I was one of the best. Looking at some of the men and women in the beds around me I realised how blessed I was.

It was all very daunting. When I arrived on Thursday 6 December, a four-month stay stretched in front of me, so I was thrilled to learn that evening that many patients were allowed to go home at weekends. I was extremely lonely for my family, and became very excited at the thought that I might be able to take a break from hospitals and the rehab, and get back to Galway. When I enquired, a nurse asked me if I had been home since my accident. I said 'Yes', which was a bare-faced lie. I just wanted the chance to get home.

I was so looking forward to getting home and Mandy came up for me early the following afternoon. I was brought out to the car in a wheelchair. I had learned how to use a transfer board in St Finbar's Ward, to go from the bed to the wheelchair, and now I was going from wheelchair to car. I was still very much a novice at it. It often took a long time, and sometimes I failed.

I was still trying to be as positive as I could, to keep my mind strong and my mood optimistic. However, that first weekend the reality of my situation hit me hard. We were living in my grandmother's old farmhouse, beside my parents' house, while we built our new home. I had been given a generic wheelchair to use, which was wide because I'm a big guy, but it wouldn't fit in through the door of the house. It had already been torture getting up over the two little nips in front of the door, but now I couldn't get through it.

Dad stood me up, held on to me, and manoeuvred me through the door and onto a chair inside. Mandy folded the wheelchair, opened it up again inside the door, and I managed to get back into it. We had to do that all the way through the house until I got to the sitting room and onto a small couch. It took over half an hour to get there and that's where I was stuck all day long, with everything being done for me. I hadn't the power to get myself out again and into the chair, and it highlighted how powerless I was, and what a battle I had in front of me.

That evening I slept in the bottom bunk in the kids' room, which was a double, because it had bars that I could use to pull myself up. Mandy had brought me a takeaway as a treat. I had been eating really well up to this, as I knew if I was ever to get back on my feet I needed to be lighter. I had lost nearly 10kg, because of how I was eating, and the effort it took to do anything. However, the oily food in the takeaway went straight through me and the next morning as I pulled myself up on the bars I destroyed the bed. Even to this day my son reminds me of that. We laugh about it, but it was, and is, upsetting.

When Mandy came in I knew she was so disappointed. She was exhausted from me just being there. I was worse than any child and she had a baby to mind, and two kids, and she had to keep the grandmother's place going. She didn't need me to look after as well. She could see how positive I was trying to be, but that was such a difficult weekend. I felt it probably would have been better for them all if I had stayed in the hospital, so when I left that weekend to be driven back, I said, 'I'm probably not going to be coming back, it's too much for ye, and it's too much for me.' Or that's what I thought, but by the time the next Friday came around I really wanted to see everyone again.

I continued to come home most weekends. Some amazing people came out of the woodwork, including friends from primary school, to get me from hospital to home and back again, including Emmet Gardiner, Joe Noone, Noel Rabbitte, Paul Neary, Paulie Thompson, Niall O'Brien, Damian (Damo) Browne, Maurice Flynn and Johnny Brennan. They drove me to help take the pressure off Mandy. Noel lives in Dublin and came to see me regularly, even though he is a busy man with his own family. He brought me out and about too – I remember one place that had amazing burgers. He's a really jovial guy, full of energy, but also such a compassionate friend. He has stayed with me throughout my entire journey, and never once made me feel like an invalid.

In hindsight that first visit home helped me see how far I had to go, the journey that was ahead of me, and I went back to the NRH with a strengthened resolve. However, visits home would continue to bring some of my most difficult moments.

We needed to get the new house completed. It was a self-build, a 3,600 square-foot house I had designed with an architect from start to finish on my dad's land. It was my dream house. Everything in it was how I wanted it. I was doing all the plans, making the decisions. And that wasn't because I wanted control, it was because I was the one that was good at visualising stuff, and that just wasn't Mandy's strength. I'd sold the derelict farmhouse that had been bequeathed to me by my aunt to pay some of the business debts, and to help fund the rest of the build. Almost all the €50,000 insurance money I got from the accident would also go into the house to get it finished.

Even from the hospital I continued getting everything organised, priced, tradespeople lined up. The one thing we had to get was a tiler to come in because I couldn't get around to the shops and pick out tiles. So one weekend I was coming down and a guy who sold tiles was to come out to the house. I asked Mandy if she could organise a wooden ramp so I could get into the house – there weren't even steps up to it at that stage – so I could see the tiles in the kitchen and the ensuite and bathrooms and make the choices. But she hadn't been able to so when I arrived there were no ramps and I couldn't even get the chair up to the door because of the gravel surface. I had to put my shame aside and to physically crawl along the ground, drag my body up into the house while the tiler watched. I tore the skin off myself getting in through the door, and then I had to pull myself up, using a door handle, to get back into the wheelchair, which someone had brought inside. And then it was another challenge getting back out again. It was a horrible experience. The one thing I had asked for hadn't happened. I understood Mandy had the kids to mind, and so much else going on, but it illustrated just how dependent I was on other people. It was a bleak realisation. I don't know whether she forgot, or just didn't understand how important it was. I don't know because we never talked about it. But I felt humiliated, and so dependent.

However, I used that and other similar experiences as fuel to drive myself on, to make myself less dependent. People really don't see another person's issues, and I'm no different, though it has changed a bit now since the accident. I used this urge for independence as a driving force, to get myself better, so I wouldn't have to be relying on others to do the basic things for me.

In my first few days in the NRH there were lots of tests, performed by Dr Shane Hanratty – my rehabilitation consultant – the physiotherapists and the occupational therapists, to check things like my reaction skills, and my response to hot touch and cold touch. As soon as they started testing they realised I had some movement. My initial record had said, 'T11 ASIA Impairment Scale A Spinal Cord Injury, no movement', so that was a boost, to know I was further ahead than they thought: I was now classified as T11 ASIA Impairment Scale C. This was music to my ears. I didn't know what it meant exactly, but it was definitely good news.

I was told I was the first person in the NRH to have a thoracic injury from lifting a bench. I'm considered an anomaly. I'm not a traumatic spinal injury, like someone who has fallen from a height or had an accident. I'm not non-traumatic, like when someone gets a growth on, or infection of, their spinal cord. With most lifting-related injuries, it's the lumbar region – the lower back – that gets injured. That's why the surgeon had said I'd been so unlucky; it was because my injury was so high up my spine. Medically I don't think they can explain it, but one health professional I met believes that I had become so locked, so heavy, so inflexible – from my weight and my lifestyle and my stress – that when the pressure came on from lifting that bench, everything was so tight around the lumbar region that the pressure kept building, building, building until it released along my thoracic discs. If I had been more flexible I might have injured my lumbar region, which would have caused issues, but nothing on the scale of what I experienced.

I learned one of my most important lessons during those first few days at the NRH. One of my runners had come off and was on the floor beside me. I couldn't quite reach it, but I could have made more of an effort to get it. Mick, a health care assistant, who turned out to be one of the best guys there, came over, went down on his hunkers and picked up the shoe. As he put it on my foot he looked up at me and said: 'Now, remember, this is a rehabilitation hospital, not a care home.' As in, 'You could have got that, so get it yourself next time.' I realised he was right. That turned everything around in my head. I was there to rehabilitate to the best of my ability, not to be looked after. I realised that every little thing I did, every task I did for myself, was going to improve me. And after that I never, ever missed an opportunity to work hard. This was my life and I needed to fight for it. It was my job to get better.

The NRH team weren't satisfied that I had built up my foundation correctly, so my rehabilitation started with the basics again. And despite the unexpected movement of my big toe, any fantasy I'd had of a miraculous recovery was quickly dispelled. I was there for about two weeks when they held a meeting with my doctors and therapists, and Mandy and Dad came up. We sat around a table and they gave me their report. At this stage I had a bit more movement, I think, a little in my ankles, but at the end of the report the conclusion was 'wheelchair-bound for life'. The report also told me what I would be able to do when I left: hand-controlled driving, shower, transfer from bed to wheelchair, wheelchair to car; very basic things. I would be shown how to be as independent as possible. But I would live my life in a wheelchair. I was gutted. But as I read it I kept thinking: 'That's just *their* target for me, not *mine*.' I wanted more. I wanted to surpass everyone's expectations. I was going to demand a lot more of myself.

By 21 December, eight weeks since the day of my accident, I was able to stand on my own two feet using handrails. I came home for Christmas, but I remember very little about it, except I had a new party trick. The lads I went to school with – David and Shane Donoghue, Brian Flannery, Paul Neary, Derek Carroll, David and Martin Brady, Paulie Thompson – brought me out for a drink. We were down the back of our local, Fields' Bar, and I showed it off. I could pull myself up with my arms and hold myself in a standing position by bracing myself and locking in my core. There's a big difference between standing on your feet and moving them, but I was being extremely positive. I was now strong enough to be able to pull myself up off the wheelchair and stand unaided, and the lads thought that was impressive!

Next came walking between the rails with a brace around my left leg to stop it buckling. My right knee was probably strong enough, but my left knee wasn't. A month later I had a new party trick and I was delighted. I could walk on my Zimmer frame, but I was really slow. We were still living in my grandmother's old house and when I went home at the weekend I'd be exhausted just making my way from the kitchen to a chair by the stove – about five or six metres – and I'd still be losing balance. But it was all progress. Mandy took a video of me edging my way between rooms with Felim chanting 'Dada' in the background. As I watched it back I recalled my grandmother using her Zimmer frame in that house many years before. All I was missing was the white hair.

On our NRH ward the most mobile patients were in the three beds at the back, and that was the place to aim for. The worse you were, the further up the unit, closer to the entrance, you were, and I wasn't near the back in those first months.

After falling asleep at about three or four in the morning, I would be awake by about seven. Then it was absolute mayhem, with people waking up, waiting their turn to get out of bed into wheelchairs, trying to get a shower, queuing to go to the toilet. There was always a queue of wheelchairs for the bathrooms. Bear in mind that all of us were catheterised or incontinent, with no control over our bowels or bladder. No matter what time of day it was there was an awful smell.

Getting down for breakfast was always an ordeal. We all had to use lifts, but in the old building there were only two, and they could only fit a couple of wheelchairs at a time. You could be queueing for five minutes. When I wheeled myself into the breakfast room, I'd put my tray on my lap and fill it up. I ate plenty but I made sure I was eating healthy food – brown bread over white, plenty of fruit and veg, smaller portion sizes, less ultra-processed food. In the dining room I eventually gravitated to a group and I stuck to that group for most of the time I was there. We always had good chats.

And then the working day began. I'd have physiotherapy appointments, occupational therapy appointments, aquatic physiotherapy appointments, strength to condition appointments, sports, day outings, and various other appointments scheduled throughout the day.

If we had free time we could go up to our wards, but during the day the rooms were very quiet so I always hung around downstairs. I would go to the coffee shop and grab a coffee, or go to the dayroom, anywhere I could be social. I didn't like being on my own. I was always going around the corridors. There was a garden right in the middle of the hospital, with corridors around it, and I'd zoom around it in the wheelchair, going as fast as I could.

Lunch was another big scramble and a queue, but it was always a decent dinner; however, I could never fathom the food choices for the evenings. They would put on stuff for fries, like sausages, rashers, pudding, so I ate very little at teatime. In the afternoons I would go to the dayroom, or do extra physio work, and after tea I'd go down to the physio room, which was staffed by volunteers for a few hours, to do extra work.

The physiotherapy room was a huge hall. I had the same daily time for physiotherapy as another patient, who was a paraplegic on my ward. He had been there for about six months before me. He was there because of a cycling accident. He'd been out doing a charity cycle when someone hit the back of his bike and he went over the handlebars and broke his neck.

When I got there he could barely hold a cup. I didn't know him but I watched how hard he worked, fighting just to be able to move his fingers to grab a cup so he could suck out of a straw; so his family wouldn't have to do that for him when he got home. And I thought, if that man can fight that hard, I certainly can too. He was one of the people around me who became my inspiration and kept me driven. I took huge inspiration from his battle.

The patient who was beside me in the ward on the left-hand side was another inspiration. He helped me a lot when I arrived, got me settled in, gave me advice, and talked to me. He was a paraplegic and his attitude was amazing. Throughout the whole time I was there he was incredibly positive, even though his gains were minuscule in comparison to mine. Watching someone be so positive and mentally strong in that situation blew my mind. I could see that he and so many other patients were in a far worse condition than me. If they could keep fighting, and stay positive, so could I.

Sorcha Barry, my physiotherapist, inspired me in a different way. She motivated and encouraged me to work harder. She got me, and my mindset, and she understood that if I was given a task to do I would do it and she could leave me alone. I didn't miss any sessions.

There was inspiration everywhere, every day. In the old NRH you went down to a kitchen/dining area for meals, and there would be groups sitting together. But there were also people everywhere for whom it was a real struggle to eat and drink. They could have had their food brought up to them but they chose to come down, they were not afraid to display their disability, or their vulnerabilities. That was something I wasn't used to. In the world of sports, and of business, you don't show your vulnerabilities, and I had mastered not showing mine. So I kept the shield up inside the NRH and homed in on my physical progress. That kept me driven and motivated, but the rest of it I parked.

I always took the hardest option, the longest route, the toughest exercise. At home at the weekends I would find other ways of pushing myself. The ramp up to my office was very steep, but I'd still push myself as hard as possible to get up that ramp and through the doors and into work. I also used competition as a tool for physical recovery. There was one fella who was on the same ward as me who I spotted on my first day at the NRH, racing up the middle of the ward in his wheelchair doing wheelie spins. I thought, 'That cocky so and so'.

He would become a great friend to me in there, but on that first day I decided to use him as my competition. I told myself, 'You're going to be able to go faster and be more skilful in your wheelchair than that lad.' I continued to use him as competition, though I never told him that. He was a really sound man, a very driven man, a very determined man. He had fallen off a bridge, and unfortunately he didn't have the same outcome as I had. He was a strong man, but he hid a lot, hid any vulnerability, just like we all probably did.

Another friend on the ward had a non-traumatic injury. Unlike those of us who had been paralysed in an instant, he had sustained a spinal cord issue working on a track machine, from all the vibrations. He lost power in his legs, but he got it back within a couple of days. However, like me, he had many other debilitating issues as a result, including severe pain. Even wearing trousers was painful for him.

The three of us had a great laugh. We would play basketball in our wheelchairs and the competition would be fierce. All the sports at the NRH were faciliated by Mark Berry from the Irish Wheelchair Association, a lovely man. We only got to play wheelchair rugby once, because it got so violent. I could understand why it used to be called murder ball. You get the ball and go as fast you can, and the other wheelchairs bounce off you. We had to stop because so many people were getting knocked over. We were hitting each other so hard the chairs were flipping over, even though they were special chairs for sports. But when you put men like the three of us together, all hugely competitive, the testosterone gets high. It was win or die, that's how our heads worked. But it was brilliant. I loved it.

Wheelchair basketball is a fantastic sport. It's way harder than normal basketball and feels much faster when you are playing it. Even trying to get a basket is far more difficult. When a basketball player goes to score, they usually stop and shoot, or lay up into the basket. In a wheelchair, you're aiming as you're moving, so from where you start to when you throw it's a totally different calculation. That's the part I found the hardest. I loved the speed of racing around the court and catching and throwing. You are hit constantly by other chairs. It was such fun. It was our way of letting off steam.

I also loved playing table tennis with other patients. Everything was a competition to me. I'd see somebody doing something that

I couldn't do, and I'd use that as motivation to get there. Every opportunity I had I pushed myself. I never relented.

By early March I was up on a rollator, and using my wheelchair less and less. I could also feel I was beginning to walk more upright. I was still walking with a frame for support, but the rollator was faster and I had to have more control. A Zimmer frame isn't going to go anywhere, but this had wheels and could take off at speed, which meant I'd fall. I'd walk around in a circle with a physio holding on to me, because it could take off. When I first went on it I felt so out of control and unsteady, and that was frightening. But it was all leading on to even more progress. I used to go out to the shops using it, and I looked like an absolute idiot, but I didn't care. I fell many times, but I got myself back up.

On the outside I was very positive, because I was making progress. But all the time I was parking things. I was parking my business worries. I was parking my financial worries. I was parking my worries about the future. I just parked all the emotional and mental stuff. I don't recall being offered any psychological supports at this stage, and I certainly didn't ask for any.

We would go up to the wards for bed around 9.30 p.m. All the visitors had to be gone, and I think lights were out at 10 p.m. That's when the pain would push to the forefront and the mind would start acting up. I'd be exhausted, but I couldn't sleep, and there were so many of us in the same boat I couldn't even complain. There would be screams during the night, and other sounds. It was a daunting time. Keeping the mental stresses at bay during those nights was difficult. It was so hard to occupy my mind. Night-time is a lonely place because other people are asleep, or focused on trying to get to sleep, or watching stuff online. I was also full of drugs. And it was during that time that I did one of the stupidest things I have ever done in my life, and probably one of the main reasons I'm now divorced.

I signed up to a dating website and started chatting online to women. Looking back, my head was all over the place. I was on a lot of drugs, including morphine-based painkillers. I had never taken strong medication in my life, and had no idea about side effects or how it might affect my mind. Maybe I just wanted a distraction, and to talk to somebody who didn't realise the position I was in, that I was paralysed from the waist down. I had quickly realised that outside of the NRH people often talked to me with pity, and I really hated that. So maybe I just wanted to talk to someone who didn't know that about me? Or maybe I needed to feel affection from someone, or that I was attractive to someone? I still don't understand why I did what I did, but whatever the reason, there was no way those conversations were going to lead anywhere. Even if I could have been teleported from the NRH, I was paralysed from the waist down. There was nothing happening!

I'd try to stop, but the next thing I'd be back at it again. I was just using it as a way to escape. They'd give me their number and I'd go on WhatsApp, and they might send me voice messages. I'd sometimes even go as far as making arrangements to meet – but sure what arrangements could I be making? – and then I'd cancel. I still to this day don't know why I started it, and why I kept doing it. This was something I would never have even contemplated doing before my accident. Looking back now I can only speculate that the cocktail of drugs I was taking had altered my personality. However, I didn't realise that I was changing into someone I didn't recognise.

My stupidity was never going to end well. One weekend, soon after my triumph at moving on to the rollator, Mandy found voice notes on my phone. I had been in my parents' house, and when I came back out I could see she had my phone, and her face was a mixture of anger and hurt. She was so upset, with good reason, and I couldn't deny or excuse what I had done. That was the weekend just before St Patrick's Day, and I spent St Patrick's Day up in the NRH because she didn't want to see me again, and I didn't blame her one iota. Now it wasn't just my business that was in trouble; my marriage was too.

I think it was the day after St Patrick's Day that I first used crutches. Unlike the crutches you might get with a broken leg they had a suspension on them, and cushion and support around the forearm. I walked for about ten metres on my own without anyone to assist me. I welled up after doing that. It was something I had never thought would happen. Looking back on Instagram I can see that I marked that achievement but added: *It's been physically extremely tough going but mentally I'm a train wreck from it.* As I was building myself back up physically, everything else was collapsing around me.

That was the first time I engaged with the psychologist, Claire, at the NRH. She met with Mandy and me and tried to help us iron things out. Mandy came up and we talked, but she was putting two and two together and making five. She assumed I had been doing that kind of stuff online before the accident – I think she was recalling all the time I had spent on my phone, being distracted by the phone, answering text after text, because of the business – but I hadn't. It remains my biggest regret, but we couldn't manage to resolve anything. I didn't find the sessions very helpful, but maybe I just wasn't in the right space for it. I was blocking everything out. I was too busy concentrating on controlling my body and ignoring my mind.

INSPIRATION IS EVERYWHERE.

Two things the NRH taught me very quickly. Number one was I realised how lucky I had been, and to look around at everything I had and to appreciate it more. And the second was that inspiration is everywhere, if you choose to look in the right places. I now look at the world in a completely different light.

I love to watch great sportspeople in action, but they are not the people who inspire me. People on the sports field have a quality that they have been gifted with, that they work hard at. A gift is no good unless you work hard. But they are fully able, and they make a choice to work and train hard.

For people with disabilities, it's not a choice. They have to go over so many hurdles just to have what we perceive as a normal life, or even just to participate in sport. I am inspired by the person who has to get up out of bed in the morning and face not one, but multitudes of problems, every day of the week, every moment of every day. We should look at people like them, not with pity but with respect, and as an inspiration to us all. They are my everyday heroes.

11

OUT THE DOORS

Learning to drive with hand controls was interesting. It's included in the rehab programme, because they want you to be able to drive independently when you leave, but I was nervous that first lesson. Before I began I had to learn how to transfer myself from the wheelchair into the car. I got in the passenger side, and the instructor, Colm Caren, was in the driving seat.

He went through everything slowly, but in a way I was lucky because I'd driven all my life. This was one part of rehab I didn't have to put much thought or effort into. I was just looking forward to getting behind the wheel again, to driving myself. It was another important step to making myself independent, another way to improve. I knew as soon as I could master the controls, and get them into my own car, I'd be able to get around the place when I got home. Mobility meant inclusivity.

After about two sessions I felt comfortable. The hardest part was braking, because it is very different. You push the hand control to brake, and then pull it forward for the accelerator. It was a bit daunting but I told myself, 'This is just another way of doing it.' I was happy out, and by the third lesson I felt I had it mastered. I was confident, but there was a bit of a lag before I got my papers to say I was roadworthy. Going down home one weekend I was so keen to drive back up to Dublin myself that I forced the paperwork through before I left on the Friday. It was another pivotal moment in my recovery.

I was in the NRH for four months, and I have nothing but praise for the staff and all they did for me. It was full of fantastic people like Dr Shane Hanratty, physiotherapist Sorcha Barry, Esther O'Driscoll, who looked after the dining room, the dayroom and the entertainment, occupational therapist Sharon McLoughlin, and Mark Berry from the Irish Wheelchair Association, who organised sports. Three of the older aides, Colm, Mick and Dave, were among the people who kept spirits high, always smiling, always helping someone out. There was always a bit of banter and they made everything as easy as possible.

I also made some great friends among the patients. On Thursday nights a group of us would go down to Baker's Corner pub, about a kilometre away, for a few drinks. We weren't meant to, but we'd 'sneak out' in our wheelchairs after a hard week's work. It was grand going down along Rochestown Avenue because there was a slight hill, but coming back was torture because we would have two or three drinks in us, and we still hadn't mastered long distance in a wheelchair. One of our gang had a motorised wheelchair, so I would grab the back of his chair, and someone else would grab the back of mine, and so on, and we'd go back as a train!

One night our pal with the motorised wheelchair wasn't with us for some reason, so there was no engine for our train. A brain injury patient, who was a small lad, but who could walk, was pushing one of the girls in her wheelchair, but when he went to put the wheelchair up on the footpath he missed the ramp up by a mile, the chair bounced back and the girl ended up on the ground in the middle of the road and hurt her knee. He started howling. He should have been able to pick her up, but he was distraught, so the only other person who could walk went down to stop the traffic. So myself and another of the lads were left, in our wheelchairs, trying to pick her up and get her back in her chair. It was comical. We were a sight, and the laughing didn't help a bit. She had to hide her injuries when we finally managed to get back.

After that people were afraid to go out again for a while, but at this stage I could drive, so we would put a kitty together and I would drive up to Lidl and buy some drinks, and we would smuggle them into the dayroom. Where there's a will there's a way, and after all we had been through we definitely had the will. We were breaking the rules, but those nights out, and in, were good craic, and a chance for us to let off steam, which we all needed.

The outings to Baker's Corner eventually resumed. Often they would be a chance to celebrate someone's 'graduation', someone going home, like the night before a lovely lady from Cork left. That night, however, a guy with a brain injury, I think possibly from drug abuse, got really drunk and caused mayhem in the pub. The drink, his medication and the brain injury were a terrible mix. It was chaos and we had to get him escorted out. And that was the end of our outings.

I'm still in touch with some of the others who were in the NRH with me. They will be friends for life. I didn't realise at the time how much easier it was to be with peers, with people who were also rehabilitating after injuries. You could talk about your physical problems and issues, and the others would understand, because we were all going through the same thing.

The better you got, the further down the ward you moved, and towards the end of my stay my two closest friends on the ward and I were down there together and we had great fun, but when first one and then the next was discharged I felt very lonely, and during my final weeks I spent very little time in the ward.

I had stopped going home because of what I had done. Mandy didn't want me there, and I couldn't blame her, but being at the NRH when most people had gone home, when it emptied out, was particularly hard. I realised then that one of my close friends was always there too at weekends, but I didn't tell him, or any of the others, what was going on with my marriage and why I was staying up in Dublin.

The physical work for rehab was my release, but any waking moment when I wasn't working, or concentrating on recovering physically, my head would go straight back into a spiral about my marriage, my business, and worrying about my family. My brain felt like it would explode. I was in a bad place but people didn't see that. Not going home at weekends was adding to my upset, my loneliness, my anger. One Saturday I decided I just didn't want to be there any more. I had no more fight in me.

I drove out to Dún Laoghaire pier. I don't remember how I got onto the pier, but I do remember looking out over the edge and bawling my eyes out. All I could think of was that in chatting to women online I had done something unfixable. My marriage was unfixable, my business was unfixable, my mind was unfixable. And then for some reason I thought I couldn't do it without leaving a note. I drove away from the pier and back up the road that leads to Dún Laoghaire's main street. I parked in a disabled bay, got out my rollator, and eventually got myself up into the Forty Foot bar that overlooked the harbour, which was really difficult because there were steps.

I bought a drink and started writing. There were lots of comings and goings, and sports on TV, but I spent about two hours over that one drink writing letters to my children, to Mandy, to my parents. I also wrote notes to two companies because I was so angry. At this stage I believed that everything that had happened over the previous few months was down to losing a contract with Citylink; that had been the catalyst for all the stress, all the extra pressure, all the hassles with employees. The loss of the Trafalgar contract had been the final nail in my coffin.

I went back down to the pier, planning to leave the letters in the car, but something stopped me, and I didn't go through with it. Maybe I still held onto the hope that I could save my marriage. Maybe I just hadn't reached rock bottom yet.

I don't recall what I did when I got back to the NRH that day, and I never told anybody about what I had thought about doing, not even my rehab psychologist, who we were still having sessions with at the time. I kept those letters for a long time before eventually getting rid of them, because they were awful things to have around.

I have a better understanding now of how hard it can be to control the mind, how dangerous it can be, how dark it can get. We all use different mechanisms to keep our mind under control and I began to realise that mine is keeping occupied. That's what I did, and what I still do now. I can't let my mind wander. If I let my mind wander it gets dangerous, so I keep myself busy.

So I said nothing about how I was feeling, but put my focus

back on the physical side of things. Physically I was smashing everything in front of me, I was knocking everything out of the park, and that's what kept me sane. Every day I worked my ass off. My mantra was 'Every day is a day to improve. Don't waste that day.' The physio room was open from six to nine o'clock every night, staffed by volunteers. I went down there most nights and I worked. Several times I was full sure I had broken bones when I fell and my legs got caught in things, but luckily I hadn't. I was so focused and driven that I wasn't afraid. As far as I was concerned it couldn't get any worse.

Two weeks prior to discharge there was another meeting with family, medical and therapy staff – I think Mandy did come up for that. But even though I was on crutches at this stage, and now classified as a T10 ASIA Impairment Scale D SCI – a huge improvement since admission – at the end of the report the conclusion/prognosis was: 'functional around the house, wheelchair-bound in public'. Even though I had made huge progress, it felt like the medical world was still knocking me back. I left that meeting and almost immediately afterwards went into my physiotherapy session with Sorcha, who had been sitting around the table. I was fuming, and I said to her, 'I'm going to walk out of here. I don't care what they say.' And fair play to her, she said, 'Let's try it.'

I have always wanted to try to prove people wrong, even from the days I played rugby with Monivea when I wanted to prove to people that you could play for a small club and still play for the Irish under-18s. With soccer it was the same thing. I was big and heavy, but I was one of the fittest on the team, even though I was only a goalkeeper. I was always pushing myself, and that was often to prove people wrong. So from the first time I was told that I was going to be paralysed for life, and to get used to it, to get my head around it, something inside me just said, 'That, now, is a challenge. I'm not going to be told I can't do something.' I don't think I realised immediately when I set out on this journey why I was taking up that challenge, but what I discovered about myself during the journey is that that's what I do; I try to prove people wrong.

When Dr Cullen told me that it might be involuntary spasms when my toe moved, I wanted to prove him wrong. When that first NRH report said, 'wheelchair-bound for life', it got me saying 'I'm going to prove you wrong.' I use what I perceive as other people's negativity as a massive driving force. So when that final report concluded I would be 'wheelchair-bound in public', I took that as a negative vibe towards me. I thought: 'I'm on my feet now, and you said I wouldn't be. I may not be walking unaided, but I am on my feet, and I'm doing more than you ever expected me to.' I left that meeting determined to prove that conclusion wrong.

In those last few weeks at the NRH I worked and worked and worked. I progressed on to the crutches, to walking a couple of metres on my own, to walking around the courtyard. I was stumbling, not walking, but I was on my own two feet.

When it came to 28 March, exit day, discharge day, nobody came up. I chose to walk out of the doors of the NRH on my own, with Sorcha beside me and another physiotherapist videoing me. I stumbled down the ramp. Sorcha was probably terrified, but I insisted. I just put one foot down as an anchor, and then the other, and kept doing that. I couldn't feel my feet touching the ground, but I could see them.

Eventually I got to the end of the ramp. The car was at the bottom, with my wheelchair in the boot. I stumbled on the bonnet, managed to get myself in, and I drove off! No fanfare, nothing. From the outside my positivity was as high as you can get. I had beaten the prediction that I would never walk again. I had used my inner drive to prove people wrong. I had walked out of the hospital.

Instagram, April 2019

I'VE DONE IT.

My journey in the @nrh_fdn has finally come to an end. What an amazing place it truly is. I have had the most amazing team working with me. A huge thank you must go to Sorcha my physio who is such a wonderful person and so great at what she does.

Honestly sometimes I think it can be so beneficial to set a target that can be out of reach. That is what I've done from week to week and it's got me walking back out of the NRH doors on my feet unaided.

NOW TO MY NEXT JOURNEY, MY FAMILY TIME

DON'T ACCEPT DEFEAT.

I was told I would never walk again. However, I chose not to accept that prognosis, or to let it define me. I chose instead to stay positive, to challenge myself whenever possible, and to focus on small victories; the tiniest movement, sitting myself up in bed, putting my feet on the ground … until eventually I walked. If you give up on yourself and accept defeat you will never move forward.

12

BABY STEPS

I didn't drive straight home. I had to stop off at IKEA in Ballymun on the way, before I headed west. Even though it wasn't ready – the staircase still hadn't been finished – Mandy had moved into the new house with the kids. I folded up the rollator and used the trolley as my support. I did get some looks, but I managed it all on my own, though I had to take breaks. I bought plants, soap dishes, glass jars for cornflakes, plates, rugs for the sitting room … all the kind of stuff that was needed to fill up the house and take away the bare look.

That took me a few hours, and the drive home was another couple. Things between Mandy and I were not good, and I don't remember what sort of reception I got when I finally reached the house, but she had said she was going to allow me to stay with them, and see if we could work through it, which was great.

I stayed in one room and she stayed upstairs. They say the worst silences are the silences when people are around, and that's what it was. To give Mandy credit, she did what she had to do to help me out, but otherwise I was on my own.

Just before I left the NRH, I'd been asked to be part of the NRH team at the Inter Spinal Unit Games in Stoke Mandeville, England. So within days of coming home I was on my way back to Dublin to meet the rest of the team at Dublin airport: assistants, physiotherapists and fellow competitors.

Stoke Mandeville Hospital and its National Spinal Injuries Centre (NSIC) are renowned worldwide as the birthplace of the Paralympic movement. It was there, back in July 1948, on the day of the opening ceremony of the London Olympic Games, that Professor Sir Ludwig Guttmann organised the first competition for wheelchair athletes to take place. Initially known as the Stoke Mandeville Games, that first competition saw 16 injured servicemen and women take part. So you can imagine how excited I was about being asked to go along to compete against other rehabilitation hospitals, from England, Wales and Scotland. It was a competition – which I always loved – and they wanted me to compete as much as I could. In my mind the tournament was all about treating people with disabilities as equals, giving us the opportunity to compete and do as well as we could.

I was on the crutches, but could only walk a very short distance, so I brought the rollator with me. I was more mobile than most of the team. However, right from the airport it was a real eye opener at how the world treats people with disabilities. It took an incredible amount of time to get us all through the airport, and I felt that those in wheelchairs were being treated as second-class citizens, being left hanging around waiting, being made to feel that they were an inconvenience, that everything was an ordeal for staff. One of my friends who was in a wheelchair was feeling nervous about the flight and he had to be put on the plane first, lifted down the aisle, and put in his seat on his own. He couldn't move until he was lifted off at the other end, and they left him sitting on that plane for ages waiting for assistance to come.

Despite this, I was so looking forward to the competition. I believed that because it was all about showing that people with disabilities are equal, we were going to be treated like athletes, albeit athletes with disabilities. I had experience from my playing background of how athletes should be treated, of how people should be treated. However, when we finally got to Arrivals there was no bus waiting for us, and when it finally came it couldn't accommodate us all properly. But we made do. There was no way this would have happened to another team in the green of Ireland, or that it would have been tolerated. Most of the others didn't seem bothered by the disorganisation as much as I was. But this was the home of the Paralympics, and I would have expected far more. Our team was put into dormitories like a boarding school with competitors from Wales and Scotland. They were the soundest of people, but it was still strange to be sharing dorms at our age, as if we were back on the ward.

I felt that even an under-14 rugby team would have been treated better. We were left in the dormitory, and it seemed that we had been forgotten about, until someone finally came to tell us where the food was, and that the sports would start the next day. Meanwhile, it was already apparent that the toilet facilities were shocking. Not only had we to queue for ages, but the smell was terrible, and they weren't maintained or cleaned properly during our stay.

The next big shock for me came the following morning. Breakfast was a big greasy fry, and all I could think was, 'We're meant to be competing today and they're serving us this! That's not how athletes are treated.' I couldn't figure out the thinking process behind it all.

It was all so demoralising. I was only a week out of hospital and was already keenly aware that I had issues getting in and out of my own house, and managing day-to-day tasks, so I had been looking forward to coming, not just to compete, but to be somewhere that treated people with disabilities with dignity and was designed to make their lives easier and better. I was so disappointed.

It was absolutely amazing to walk into the sports complex and see a huge mural of Dr Guttmann, and all his achievements. It was really impressive, but was what we were experiencing doing justice to that man's legacy? Would he have been happy with it?

Even when it came to the sports, so much of it was disorganised. There didn't seem to be a proper timetable. We were kept waiting around in the cold for hours and nobody in my competitions, which included wheelchair tennis, snooker, table-tennis, golf and power-lifting, seemed to know what was going on or where it was going on. I felt that this level of disorganisation would not have happened at any level of able-bodied athletics or sports. It was a shambles. I hadn't played wheelchair tennis in the NRH, but I won all my games. However, when it came to the semi-final I was kept waiting for so long that I gave up and went off. Others on the team had a more positive experience, but I had got myself into a mindset that it was all awful. I gave up waiting for my events and headed to the pub.

I had wanted to thrive, to compete, but I found it all very demoralising and upsetting, and I just didn't want to do any part of it. It was so disheartening and worrying that this was how a hospital and organisations that worked with disabilities organised an event. If this was how they looked after people, what chance did we have out in the real world? I kept thinking, 'If this is what's ahead of me, what can I look forward to?' It was such a bad message to be sending out. Knowing what people with disabilities have to put up with, what they are expected to put up with and be satisfied with every day, is a huge driver for me. I will continue to call that out. It's just not right.

When I got back home Mandy continued to avoid me at every opportunity, which wasn't easy, as once I was inside the house I couldn't leave. The steps at the back and the front still weren't done, and getting in and out was a huge challenge. I did it when I absolutely had to, but at times I felt like I was a prisoner in my own home. I'd watch TV and the kids would come and spend time with me, but obviously they would have to go to bed, and the nights were so long, so quiet and so very difficult. I was in my space and Mandy was in hers. And I do not do silence well.

I now understand what I found so difficult about that time, why it drove me cracked. Since the accident I had faced a series of challenges and I had met them. I had set myself the challenge of walking out of the NRH and that was what had kept me focused. Every day was a day to improve. But when I got home I had no challenges to focus on. My body was still failing me. My business was almost gone, and now it looked like my marriage was almost gone too. There was nothing to cling on to, nothing to drive me, nothing to keep my mind busy.

I had used the symbolism of walking out the doors of the NRH as a goal to reach. I had beaten the predictions and had left there on a high. However, after a few days at home, reality struck. I was back on my feet but I still couldn't pick up my son in my arms and take a step. I couldn't make a cup of tea and bring it from one table to the next without spilling it. I still had to master going up and down stairs. Because I have no proprioception – the ability to sense where your body is in relation to what's around you – I was losing my balance very easily. All I could do was stand on my feet and take a few steps on level ground; anything more than that, and I was gone. It was clear that I still had so much further to go, so much further that I could go. I wasn't prepared to accept that this was going to be my limit.

Any hope of living a normal life seemed so far off. It was daunting to even figure out just how I was going to improve and achieve a better quality of life. But I decided I would continue to build on what the NRH had taught me, and how they had taught me. I had left without a programme. They told me I was making so much progress that they didn't want to give me one in case it slowed me down. So I decided the simplest way to keep up the progress was to get back into a gym. I hadn't been in one in years.

Usually, I look for the hardest option, as it makes me feel even better when I succeed. However, this time I knew I had to take the sensible option. I joined a gym that had a swimming pool, a lift, and was as accessible as possible. Right beside the entrance of the gym there was a wheelchair lift and a ramp down. So for the first month after I got home, I used the wheelchair. I would get myself up to the gym and I'd start work.

At the NRH the process was to try to complete and master a movement first in the water, in aquatic physiotherapy, so it was not weight-bearing. I decided to continue that method. The first thing I would do was get myself into the pool and try a movement, repeating it over and over; maybe lifting my legs a little higher and getting the rotation going, or taking a tiny step up. Then I'd shower and go up to the gym. There I'd repeat the movement I had been practising in the pool. I'd hold on to a machine and I'd lift my leg high and hold it; lower it; lift it high and hold it. Everything was about control, being slow and controlled. Then I would put a mat on top of a mat, which still wouldn't be more than a few inches high, and I'd step up on to the mat, and down, up on the mat, and down. I wouldn't take weight off one of my legs, I'd just be going through the motion of load-bearing. And I'd do that hundreds of times. I'd fall on a regular basis, but I kept getting back up, and continuing that mundane task of trying to take a step; hundreds and hundreds and thousands and thousands of times with each foot. I did a lot of work on my glutes, because they are so important to keep you stable; even just sitting on the floor and lifting my pelvis upwards. Everything I did I started at the very lowest level.

I accepted that it was all a process, that it was going to take a lot of time and effort. I did get frustrated at times, but I could see the progress. I could see it coming, and that kept me driven and focused. It also helped me shut out everything else that was going on. It was just sheer determination to improve, to get the physical part right.

Another exercise I did was to lie down on my back, pull my knees up, and put my feet underneath my knees, so they looked like a triangle. An able-bodied person's knees would stay pointing up to the sky, but mine were flopping out. I would put a plastic cup on top of my knee, open side down, and concentrate on keeping the knee stable enough to hold that cup. I would hold my knee stable for as long as I could, until the cup fell off. Then I would do it with the other knee. That was exhausting, but it was working on getting control back in my muscles to hold my legs still. If I wasn't concentrating fully, my legs would wobble all over the place. The cup was to help me concentrate. The other leg would be flopping around, but I just concentrated on the knee with the cup, working the muscles to keep it stable, by holding it as long as I could. When you don't have sensation in your legs, when you don't have the feeling, doing that is so different. The cup would keep falling off and I'd pick it up and start over again.

In another exercise I would fill a basin with water, put marbles in it, and place an empty basin beside it. I would put my foot in and try to pick up the marbles using the gaps between my toes. Trying to do that when you have no feeling is very hard. You eventually pick up a marble – it takes a long time to master this – and you move your foot and drop it into the other basin. It is all just about regaining control of your muscles, prompting your muscle memory.

The vast majority of things I can do now are mechanical. They have been taught into me, and I am still constantly teaching my body new movements for situations it hasn't met, or been taught, since the accident.

Everything I did was at the slowest pace you can imagine, and then I would also be trying to strengthen my core at home. Stretching was, and is, still really important because even before the accident I was very inflexible. Now I can stand on my toes, which I wasn't ever able to do before. I can bend down, touch the ground with my hands and stand on my fingers with my knees straight. I'm a lot more flexible now than I used to be, because I now understand the importance of it.

After about three weeks I got rid of the wheelchair and got myself in and out of the gym without it. I was still falling over three or four or five times a day but I had my fall perfected. When I'd tip over, I'd be nearly on the way back up by the time I'd hit the ground, because I had mastered the momentum. I knew the momentum would swing me back. Whereas if I didn't get up straight away, I'd have to nearly climb up against a wall, or get my feet from underneath me and look for something to grab on to to pull myself up. With momentum, if I fell, I just rolled with it and kind of pushed my hands up off the ground and got back up.

Now I always parked well away from the door of the gym, so I'd have to get myself to the door as well. That was tough, but it was the hard option, which always led to a vast improvement. Every hour I worked was an hour gained, not an hour wasted. My rugby friend Damo Browne came and showed me how to optimise my time in the gym, how to do drills, how to build myself up. I enjoyed those sessions and they really helped me. I was working all the time, not just in the two and a half hours I was spending in the pool and gym every day. If I was standing waiting for the kettle to boil, l would put my hand on the countertop and do some squatting movements, maybe I'd only go down millimetres at first, but day by day I would improve. And I kept making and carrying that cup of tea until I could manage it.

I would go into the supermarket, which was Joyces' at the time, with a basket on my little rollator, and walk around to do the shopping. I'd be so tired sometimes I'd have to turn around and sit back into the rollator, or I would have fallen down. My legs were all over the place, turned out, and some people might have been embarrassed to be seen like that, but my mindset was that doing this shopping would improve me.

When the banisters were finally on the stairs, I'd challenge myself to go up on my bum backwards and then I'd walk from one side of the landing to the other and back, holding on to the banisters. The biggest difficulty was controlling myself coming back down the stairs. Eventually I got to the stage where I could take steps along the landing without holding on to the banisters. Every opportunity I had to retrain my body, and improve it, I took. It didn't matter where I was. I knew there was no flooring in the master bedroom's walk-in wardrobe, and money was short. So, sitting on my bum, I dragged myself and some old carpet clippings upstairs, and I spent the day putting down that bit of carpet. Even the action of sitting down on my hunkers and pulling the carpet up the stairs was training. Everything I did in that period was to make myself better. I even used the steps on the buses in the yard to train my leg movements, and they are high, particularly that first step.

I was also doing things to keep my mind occupied. I was staying in the guest room, where a lot of the furnishings were black, so I decided to paint the side lockers and the bedframe black to match. Now that's a grand idea for a normal person, they'd take the bed apart and bring it down to the yard, and it would all be done in a day. I got help with getting the bed and lockers out, but it took me a few days to paint them. To stand upright, to hold my balance and remain on my feet was physically exhausting. Every time I had to change position to paint another small section I would have to readjust myself, and try and hold my balance in that new position. It was incredibly tedious, but it was another exercise. Just staying on my feet while I painted that furniture was a mission, so it was helping me improve, re-teaching my body ways to hold itself upright. I was trying to do as much as I could to make myself less dependent. It also helped me eat up time, to distract me from the increasingly dark thoughts.

TAKE THE HARDEST ROAD.

During and after my rehabilitation I always took the hardest road for every physical task. In my mind, if I succeeded at an easy task I would still have many more to do. However, if I failed to complete the harder tasks, I knew I would still have made huge gains, and greater progress.

13

HITTING THE BOTTOM

It is still hard to reconcile my euphoric departure from the NRH to my total mental collapse within a few weeks. The timeline of a lot of what happened in those months after I left the NRH still gets jumbled in my head. I was taking a lot of medication, including oxycodone, and there is still a lot of memory loss from the time, but there were so many factors.

Fatigue was really getting to me. I still couldn't sleep properly and the pain was relentless and unforgiving. I had been working hard on my physical progress, but mentally I was crashing. My marriage was in tatters. The business was crumbling. Finance companies were putting a lot of pressure on me, but I kept that to myself. Mandy had never been involved in the business and wouldn't want to know about it.

Something had to give. In the end it was a small thing that tipped me over the edge. It was a lovely May day and my dad was building a block pillar in the farmyard, which was right beside the sun room in the house. He was outside with his shirt off, and I was sitting inside surrounded by our lovely new furniture. But I couldn't even manage to get up, lean on the couch to open the window and say hello to him. I felt like a prisoner in my own house. The steps still hadn't been done and there was no ramp. To get outside was a massive mission. I sat there brooding, thinking, 'I'm a strong thirty-nine-year-old man, and my sixty-eight-year-old dad is outside building a pillar on his own, and I can't even say hello to him.' It was like something died inside me. All I could think was: 'I'm useless. Physically, I'm useless. Mentally, I'm useless. I'm no good to my wife. I'm no good to my kids.' I gave up. I had no more fight in me.

I knew I needed to get out, to get away, and I remembered Willie Parker, a good friend of mine from rugby, was having a stag party in Limerick. He had invited me to go but I had said I wouldn't because of my condition. So I rang him up and said 'I'm coming.' I rarely drink at home, but I did that day, and I drove down drinking beers. When I got to Limerick I lost myself in drink. First I met Joe Noone, but I never let on to him what was going on for me. I didn't even let the elation of urinating on my own, without a catheter, for the first time give me a lift. I ruined that lovely moment by going to the stag party and making an absolute ass of myself. I drank myself into a terrible state. All I cared about was my own sorrow, my own misery, and I must have been awful company. Then arriving back at the hotel I fell over getting out of the taxi, because my legs still weren't good, and I had to crawl into reception. They thought I was drunk and out of control, and called the guards on me, which made me even angrier. When I woke up in the morning I had wet the mattress because of my lack of bladder control. That was a moment in my life I don't want to relive too often. I was such a mess in every shape and form.

I got up and drove home to Athenry. When I got back to the house Mandy was bundling the kids into the car, and when I said 'Where are you going?' she said 'Just going'. In hindsight I can't blame her. I was toxic, but I didn't see that at the time. I was so toxic, so angry, that if she had said black I would have said white.

I must have been a nightmare to be around. But all I could think was: 'Fuck this, I don't want to be here any more.'

I managed to get myself into the house – there were cement blocks to one side of the door and I could pull myself up onto those and over the door lintel by grabbing onto the door handle and frame. I don't know how long I was inside but I made my decision. I would go into Galway city and throw myself off a bridge on the River Corrib, a bridge that was a notorious suicide spot.

Getting out of the house was even more difficult than getting in. I had to let myself fall onto the floor, and then manoeuvre my legs outside and onto the ground, and lever myself upright with my crutches.

I sped off towards Galway. There's a railway bridge near our house that has very bad bends, you need to be careful on it, but I drove across that bridge at 50 miles per hour. I didn't care what happened to me, or anyone else. I still don't know how I didn't crash.

Something must have clicked, my subconscious must have been trying to stop me, because I went over to my cousin Derek's house, who would be like a brother to me and a really important person in my life. Like myself, he's a man who wouldn't know how to deal with a moment like that, but that's who I went to, that's who I wanted to be with. I was in a terrible state, and he kept trying to console me. I just kept repeating, 'I'm gone. I'm gone.' Derek tried to reassure me that everything would be alright, and I'm sure he tried to stop me, but I got back in the car and continued to Galway. At this stage either my parents or my sister had called into the guards, saying they thought I was suicidal and could they help find me. So unbeknownst to me there was an alert put out.

When I arrived into Galway the tide was only coming in. That meant the water was very low and if I had thrown myself over the bridge I would have hurt myself further, but not drowned. However, I was determined to finish it this time. I decided to wait for the tide, and I went to a pub I had never been to before. There was a crowd in there having great craic but I just put my head down. I drank two pints. I never even thought about writing a note.

I had never believed in stress and anxiety. I had never understood how somebody could take their own life, could let things get that deep. I do now. I was so engulfed in my own sorrow I didn't think of the repercussions for anybody else. I used to wonder how people could do that to their kids, their partner, their parents. But you get to the stage where you don't even think about them, or what it might do to them, except that you are no good for them. You don't think about anyone else, let alone care about them; that's where your mind is when you want to end your life.

I left the pub when I knew the tide would be in. I was headed back towards the bridge, and was just 200 metres away, and fully intent on killing myself, when out of the corner of my eye I saw a car pull up across the street. Someone ran across the road. It was a garda, a guy I hadn't seen in 10 or 12 years. I had played under-18s Connacht rugby with Ger Brady, and he had recognised me. Another garda in that car would not have known me, but it was Ger, and he did. He pinned me up against the wall and said, 'What are you at, man?' At that moment it felt like everything just drained out of me. Ger Brady saved my life. I thanked him afterwards, but not enough. It can never be enough.

They took me in to Mill Street Station, and Ger contacted my sister, and my parents, and some of my close friends. He orchestrated who came in to me and kept Mandy out because he knew the situation. He did such a brilliant job making sure I was minded and had the right people with me for that very dark moment in my life, even though I couldn't look them in the face. Derek Carroll and I had been friends since we were toddlers. For some reason he never got up to me in the NRH, but it was Derek who was the first friend in the station with me. I don't recall much about those hours in Mill Street, but I knew he was shocked and worried by what I had tried to do. It was such a comfort having him there beside me. Attracta was brilliant too, even though she was obviously devastated. She is all about family and has always been a great support.

Then there was talk about what to do next, and I was being told, 'Maybe you should go into a psychiatric ward. If you sign yourself in, you can sign yourself out tomorrow.' I was sold a bit of a pup there, but it was the best pup I was ever sold. I went into the psychiatric ward at University Hospital Galway.

I talked to someone briefly that night, and the next morning I spoke to a team, who I assume included a psychiatrist and a psychologist. When I went to sign out the next morning they told me I wasn't deemed well enough, or safe enough, to sign out. I was extremely pissed off at first, and very angry for the first few days, but I soon realised this was where I needed to be.

The unit was a tough place to be. I was in a ward with guys who were obviously long-term psychiatric patients, and there were other young men in there too. I think I had one hour of visiting time every day. Mandy came in, and Noel Rabbitte and Joe Noone, Attracta and my dad. I don't recall much about those conversations. I had no access to my phone; I had to do a lot of talking, and a lot of thinking. I would keep out of the other patients' way in a tiny courtyard, where I would occupy my time by doing laps to improve my walking. I was put on antidepressants, and ultimately, the conclusion was that I was full of anger; full of anger at life, at everything. All this was just a few weeks after getting out of the NRH. That's how quickly it had all turned around. I had gone from the euphoria of beating the prediction that I would never walk again to pacing the courtyard of a psychiatric ward after planning to kill myself.

I needed to find out what had brought me here. I realised I had fallen down a ladder that had brought me to this point, and if I went back up that same ladder I would end up back in the psychiatric unit again. I was finding out an awful lot about the brain and how it worked, and I knew I needed to start looking at where I had gone wrong, and to start making changes.

I could see the business was gone, but that was now out of my control. I had to start to look at what I could control. I began to think about things a bit more positively. I asked myself when I had been happiest in my life and realised that was probably between the ages of 16 to 24 or 25. People might say, 'Sure everybody's happy when you're young, you're out having a good time.' But it wasn't just that. That was the era in my life when I had the time to make relationships with people. I'm a social person. There was no social media in those days; you went out to meet people, you played sport. You hung around afterwards. You spent time with people, and you got to know people, really got to know people. That's what made me happy.

When you're playing sports, you have time to be social, to develop relationships and create relationships, to be part of the unit, part of the team. Even though I had been going to the gym since the accident, I wasn't being social. I was keeping to myself, I was missing out on that vital social connection that I needed. I was missing out on human relationships. So I said, 'Right, I need to replicate that when I get out of here. I need to start making time for people, for my relationships again.'

And then I began to think about what motivated me, what made me tick. When I was figuring that out it dawned on me that everything I'd done in my life was always about challenges and creating competition. When I picked cabbages for my dad, I wanted to be the first one to have 100 bundles picked. If I was running down the road after cows I wanted to be the one who got them in the gap first. When I played rugby, I was never happy just playing with my team. I always wanted to try to get further, and it was the same with soccer. And then when I came to be in business, I was never happy to just be the medium-sized bus company. I wanted to be the best.

I tried to figure out why I had often felt content since the accident, despite being paralysed, despite my business troubles. And it dawned on me that for all those months I had given myself a challenge – every day was a day to improve. I had never felt more content than when I was determined to walk out of the NRH. Creating challenges and competitions, even in my own head, had kept me driven and focused, and distracted from my troubles. I realised I needed a new challenge to occupy my mind.

At that stage, I would have been able to walk only three or four laps of that courtyard, which was maybe 50 metres long and 15 or 20 metres wide, before I'd have to sit down and rest. But I said to myself, 'It's almost five months now from the anniversary of the accident. To mark that anniversary, I'm going to walk from where the accident happened back through the doors of the NRH, and I'm going to fundraise for the NRH Foundation, though what the NRH did for me can never be repaid.'

I didn't even know how long the distance was from Athenry to the NRH because I didn't have my phone to look it up. I still had to spend another day or two in the psychiatric unit, so I started walking the laps of the courtyard with a purpose, and I stayed at it. Now I had a challenge. Now I had something to focus on. Now I had a purpose. That was the first building block in remaking my fragile mind.

Those seven days in that psychiatric ward turned out to be the best seven days of my life. They saved me and helped me evolve into the person I am today. I wasn't surrounded by other distractions. I had just myself and quiet, and time, to actually concentrate on my mental wellbeing. And it worked. I figured out who I was, and what drove me. It transformed the way I look at life and helped me understand myself. I would continue to have struggles, but that was the turning point.

TAKE TIME TO UNDERSTAND YOU.

It took admission to a psychiatric ward for me to figure out what made me happy, and what motivated me. Take time out to understand who you are, what drives you, and what makes you tick and thrive. Stop trying to be someone you are not. None of us is the same.

14

FRIENDS AND A ROAD TRIP

In the months leading up to my accident I had internalised all my worries, all my stresses, and in the months afterwards I continued to make that mistake. I felt such a failure. My body had failed. My marriage was failing. My business was failing.

I kept it all inside me. I believed that as a man you don't share your feelings. It may seem simplistic, but I think the reason we don't share is because us men see ourselves as fixers. I certainly did. If I share my problem with another man, I know straight away that he's going to try to fix it. A woman might listen, might be empathetic, but they won't feel the need to fix everything for me. I felt, and still often feel, that if I share with a man, I am really sharing my burden, because he will take on my problem and try to fix it for me. We feel we are giving our burdens to somebody else to fix, and we don't want that. Everything in our DNA is geared to solve or resolve problems. I felt that the minute I shared that with my friends, I was going to be burdening them with my load.

But my friends wanted to help me carry that load, even to lift the weight off my shoulders just a little. I had two groups of friends: the friends I had gone to school with and played soccer and hurling with; and my rugby mates. The day after I left the psychiatric ward Alex Dolan, one of those rugby buddies, organised a lunch for me with himself and Damo Browne. I don't think they were there to make me dig deep, to explain myself; they wanted me to know I could lean on them.

We had lunch in a pub in Craughwell, a few miles from my home, and we talked it out. I told them the business was fucked, I was broke, my marriage was broken. This was the first they knew about all this. Sitting there, I felt supported. I knew these guys had my back, and a wave of understanding swept over me that I had people there for me, I had friends there for me.

Neither of those lads, or my other friends, had known how much I was suffering. They knew about the physical side of things, they had seen me thriving at that, overcoming so much, but they had never seen what was going on behind that facade. Nowadays we are all consumed with our own lives, because we have to be so switched on all the time, that we don't see how other people are suffering. And when we do see that someone is suffering it can almost be too late.

That was the first time I opened up to people. They listened, and they let me know they had my back. We spent a couple of hours talking, but for them to come together and do that for me felt pretty amazing.

As June began I continued my gym training and started walking more, with the challenge in mind. Then I started sharing the idea with my family and friends, and we put a committee together, including my sister Attracta, Derek Carroll, Pete Burke, John Culkin and David Brady.

The people who would help me raise the money and finish that walk were a powerful circle of support round me. I had let a lot of those relationships go, or neglected them, because I had been so busy building up the business; I had put that ahead of everything, and had no time for anything else. I ignored all these past relationships that had taken time to build. But those people came to my rescue and helped me when I needed it most.

I began by walking up and down the driveway, the boreen, up to the house, which is only maybe 200 or 300 metres. Then one day when I got to the bottom I decided I was going further. I went out onto the road and turned left. Ahead of me was a railway bridge, a hump in the road. It was daunting to go up this little hill on my own without anybody to hold me in case I fell. But I managed it; and then I went down the far side, and there was another little hill. I went as far as the old water pump at the nearest crossroads that day and I walked back again.

Every day I increased the distance, and when I had a bit more confidence, I went into Athenry town and walked around its ring road. Then, to break the monotony, I started to get the train into Galway city. From the train station in Eyre Square I'd walk all the way out to Salthill and out by the prom, and then back in again. On another day I might drive into Galway and get out at the Huntsman Hotel and walk along Lough Atalia, along the docks and out by the Salthill prom. The prom became a favourite walking place for me, because it was just so beautiful, so fresh. Some days I'd hop in – I'd have brought a bag with a change of clothes – and get into the cold water to give me another lift.

It was my fortieth birthday on 30 June. Things were bad with Mandy so I decided to do something for myself. I put it out there that I wanted to do a bit of travelling in the US and Damo said he would go with me on an American road trip. I had got €50,000 from the bus insurance for my accident, and I used a few thousand of that before putting the rest into the house, that's how I could afford it. I had also bought a cheaper car, a 12-year-old high-mileage Q7 jeep, for €3,500. I had sold my own car and cleared the finance on it.

We left just after my son's birthday on 6 July. That had been a very difficult day. Mandy had laid out a blanket on the grass at the back of the house, like for a picnic, and brought out the cake and put it on the ground so that he could blow out the candles and everyone would sing 'Happy Birthday'. But of course I wasn't able to get on the ground, I had to stand at a distance and watch the party. I would have had to struggle to get up and down and show my vulnerability and disability in front of everyone.

We flew into Las Vegas. I had planned a ten-day road trip. We went to Monument Valley, Canyonlands, Arches National Park and Bryce Canyon, with the last two nights back in Vegas. It was all absolutely amazing, just a stunning part of the world to visit. I could still barely walk and it was tough going at times. At Arches National Park, I walked out to a natural stone arch that is probably bigger than the cathedral in Galway. It was such a trek, in intense heat, and when we turned around to head back the legs just went from under me. Damo helped me back on my feet, and I eventually made my way back. Slowly. I was still weaker than I looked, or that I was prepared to accept.

Back in Vegas Damo treated me to an amazing dinner in one of the restaurants at the Bellagio Hotel, where we were staying. It was probably the best eating experience I've ever had. I don't gamble, but I loved the randomness of the Vegas casinos. You never knew who you'd get talking to. One night I started chatting to a guy at one of the casino bars, who said, 'You look like a guy who played a bit of rugby.' He was a Texan and a bit older than us, and he had played rugby in college. Then he saw Damo, the man mountain, coming in, and he was like, 'Wow!' He brought over his girlfriend, a fine-looking woman, and we had a few drinks together. He started telling us how much he loved her. 'I've been married before. She's been married before ... but I love this girl, and she doesn't know it but I brought her here to marry her. And I need somebody to stand for me.' So Damo shouts, 'We'll do it!', and the next thing we're in a taxi heading off to the White Chapel to be witnesses to the wedding. But on the way the taxi driver asked if the Texan and his girlfriend had their licence from the city council, and of course they didn't, so we ended up turning around and going back.

While we were in Vegas Damo also wanted to go to the famous XS Nightclub at the Wynn Hotel. I was very unsteady on my feet and the doorman stopped me, thinking I was drunk. When I explained I had a disability they couldn't do enough for me. It was a stark difference from Stoke Mandeville. They rolled out the red carpet, they brought me to an entrance without steps, and told me to call on them if I needed anything. I was blown away. That's how you treat somebody with a disability. The club was something else: people were jumping into a swimming pool, bottles of champagne were being brought to tables, but we were just onlookers.

People had been very nervous about me going off. It was only about seven weeks after I'd left the psychiatric ward, so it was brave of Damo to take me on. It was so good to get away from everything, to park the worries about the business, and my debts, and my family, even for just ten days.

I was still trying to make the business work, and I was also really hoping that my marriage could be saved, but I could also see that Mandy was pulling away all the time, even by doing small things like getting her own car insurance. Going on that trip was also a bad idea for our relationship, and other people warned me about that, but in hindsight I don't think it would have made any difference if I hadn't gone. Maybe I was being selfish, but getting away was really what I needed at the time to help clear my head, to put a distance between myself and my problems, even for a short time.

NO MATTER HOW BAD TIMES GET, THEY WILL EVENTUALLY MAKE YOUR GOOD TIMES FEEL EVEN GREATER.

You need to have spent time in the dark to appreciate the light.

15

A DANGEROUS COMFORT BLANKET

When I left the NRH I was taking 26 tablets a day. Among the 12 medications prescribed on my discharge letter were: gabapentin for nerve pain; tramadol for pain relief; apixaban, to prevent deep vein thrombosis; tizanidine, a muscle relaxant to prevent spasms; zopiclone, a sleeping tablet; and finally OxyNorm, a quick-release version of the opioid oxycodone.

Oxycodone works by blocking pain signals from the central nervous system and the brain to the rest of the body. It also reduces the anxiety and stress caused by pain. Its long-release formula is known as oxycontin, which I had never heard about at the time. Possible side effects of that one pain reliever alone included confusion, depression, anxiety, nervousness, difficulty in sleeping, abnormal thoughts or dreams, hallucinations, mood changes, unpleasant or uncomfortable mood, disorientation, restlessness, agitation, loss of memory, seizures, fits or convulsions, and possibly aggression!

Taking it puts you in a sort of drowsy state of semi-consciousness. The best way I can describe it is that lovely feeling when you wake up and it's cold outside, you can hear the rain lashing off the window, but you are snuggled up in a comfortable warm bed with the covers over you, and you are so cosy you don't want to get out. You feel that kind of comfort when you take oxycodone. You drift in and out of sleep. You're in another world.

There wasn't a day when I didn't take it, and I would always be looking forward to the next dose, because it was a great painkiller, as well as being addictive. I don't remember how many I would take, but certainly five or six most days.

Euphoria and feelings of relaxation are the most common effects of oxycodone on the brain. There were periods when I was just floating on cloud nine. However, I realise now that it can also cause mood swings, memory issues and even violent outbursts. The list of side effects for gabapentin, which I was taking for nerve pain, also include mood changes and memory problems. I still have zero recollection of anything I watched on TV at night in the NRH, when I couldn't sleep, and the chatting to women online is just a blur. All those nights are a haze. It's a little bit scary.

Even sitting down now and trying to sort events into a timeline for myself was one of the biggest challenges in writing this book. The sequence and detail of key moments have become all mashed up in my head: leaving the NRH, making a fool of myself at the stag party, the last big argument with Mandy.

My behaviour changed. My moods were erratic. I became volatile. I was in no shape or form the person I knew I was. I had started doing things I would never have done before; things I would never have dreamed of doing. It changed me as a person.

Drinking alcohol while you're taking oxycodone can make you feel more sleepy or increase the risk of serious side effects, but I either didn't realise that or occasionally chose to ignore it. I recently remembered another awful night, another example of where my head was at after I left the NRH, and before I was admitted to the psychiatric ward.

My best friend Paul Neary came down from Belfast to see me and get me out of the house. He picked me up to go for a few drinks in Galway city. I only had about four pints, but my walking still wasn't great, so I would have been stumbling. By the time we moved from one pub to go into the Front Door bar, I was physically exhausted but I was also getting very tired because of my medication. I was drowsy at the bar, and the barman refused to serve me, which was the right call. However, I absolutely lost it when he wouldn't serve me. I lost all control. I went crazy until eventually the bouncers pinned me to the ground. Paul was trying to tell them I was disabled, I had a spinal cord injury, because they were shouting at me to get up, and I couldn't. I hadn't the power in my legs and they thought it was because I was so drunk. Then whatever hold they had on me put so much pressure on my bladder that I urinated all over myself. The gardaí came and made it even worse, they put the handcuffs on me and were shouting at me to get up, but I couldn't, and they wouldn't believe me or Paul, because they thought we were both just drunk. Eventually they put me in the back of the van and brought me to Mill Street station, and left me in a cell for the night.

I was still roaring and shouting, telling them I needed my medication because I was in so much pain, but they wouldn't believe me, even when I finally calmed down. I think it was a female garda who finally started listening to me. I think I convinced her that I wasn't just drunk because I had the self-catheterisation bags in my jacket pocket. When they let me out in the morning my pain was through the roof.

My head was so gone that I had flipped because a barman refused to serve me a drink. I felt he had made that decision without giving me a chance to explain myself, and I was so sensitive about being a disabled person at the time. All they assumed was that I was a big strong man, pissed drunk and acting the maggot. Fair play to the owner of the bar, John Mannion; he didn't want to press charges. I had broken a window in the door, and all he asked was that I pay for the broken glass. However, I was in such a dark place that I wouldn't even go in and do that. Mandy went in and paid him. She had to put up with a lot!

It was just another example of me acting crazy. There's no hiding from that. But I think people put that down to me acting out and didn't realise it was a sign that I really wasn't doing well, that mentally I was in a very bad way.

It's very hard to describe just how all the medication made me feel. I was in another world completely, and I wasn't even aware of that. Even reading back over these last paragraphs triggers other flashbacks. I didn't know anything about oxycontin at the time. I just knew it wasn't good for me. It was only years later that I realised how dangerous it could be. I don't recall any doctor telling me that it might cause problems, or to try and get off it, because it was a great painkiller, and they knew I needed that. However, I eventually realised myself I was going down a really scary path.

In addition to being volatile, I became increasingly forgetful. I could have a full-blown conversation with my father or sister, but five minutes later have absolutely no recollection of what I had said, or what I had promised to do. I got so confused about it all. Did I really forget? Or were they pulling the piss? I would regularly deny having those conversations. To this day, I can say something and completely forget it minutes later.

I also have very poor recollection of my childhood and younger years. I find it very difficult to resurrect a memory, or talk about things from my childhood, especially in descriptive terms. Some of that long-term memory loss could be from concussions during my years playing rugby. However, I'm sure the short-term memory loss is caused by the drugs.

It says a lot about OxyNorm that I cannot remember when I finally weaned myself off taking the tablets back to back to get through the day and night. I'm not sure when I realised that I was addicted, or how much it was messing with my head, but I knew I needed to stop depending on it if I was to start getting better. I knew if I was to rebuild myself, I needed to come off it. And I finally did manage to taper off until I was only using it occasionally.

I am never relaxed because of the pain, and I know that it is with me for life. That is hard to deal with, and there are some nights, maybe once every few weeks, when I'm lying on my own and the pain is just overwhelming, all-encompassing, and it seems hopeless. I know then that the only way to get to sleep, or endure the pain, is to take an OxyNorm. I take it hoping that maybe after an hour I might start to drift off, and when I wake up an hour or two later the pain might have reduced. However, I will never take them back to back, or one night after another, no matter how bad it gets. Having to live with that pain every moment of your life can get very tough, but the only alternative is to take oxycodone. And that would mean that once again it would mess with my mind, I would not be the same person. So I would rather deal with the pain than become a completely different animal to the one I really am. I put up with the pain, 24/7, because I have to, or the drugs would eat me up.

WE ALL MAY NEED CRUTCHES AT DIFFERENT STAGES IN OUR LIFE.

But there will also be a time when it's important to drop those crutches and move on by ourselves.

16

THE TOUGHEST TREK

When I told the NRH about my plan for a walk to mark my anniversary, they called me to a meeting. They sat me down with John Lynch, Éimear Smith, who is a runner herself, and I think Sorcha was there as well. I wanted to attach the NRH Foundation as a chosen charity. I wanted to raise money for them. However, they asked me not to do it because they thought it wasn't possible, the year after my accident, to walk 206 kilometres across the country. They asked me not to do it because I did not realise what I was going to be putting my body through. At this stage I could still only walk about 700 metres without having to take a rest.

But by the end of that meeting I think they understood better what drove me, and they knew I wasn't going to take their advice. I was determined to complete the challenge, which I'd already named: The Toughest Trek. It was interesting to see that they knew my character at this stage. They knew that if I put my mind to something it's hard to stop me. And once again, I used my constant drive to prove people wrong as a massive motivation to complete the challenge. I also knew this challenge would keep me focused on my continued recovery.

Our committee met every week and I continued my own training. I started going places for training walks to build awareness about the challenge. I went out to Carna in Connemara, where my mother is from, and met up with Kevin Ward. Some of the Clifden and Connemara All Blacks teams came and joined me on a walk up by the Alcock and Brown landing site. That was very beautiful.

The rugby community was phenomenal in getting behind me. Connacht Rugby even brought me out at half-time in a match to tell the crowd about the Toughest Trek, and to get the word out about my GoFundMe page. It proved to me that with the rugby community – and it really is a community – when it hits the fan, they are there for you. I had been involved for a short time on the Competitions Committee with Adrian Leddy, from Creggs RFC. I had no affiliation with Creggs but Adrian was retiring from the Irish Farmers' Association, and he donated the money raised at his IFA retirement dinner in Roscommon to my walk. It was an unbelievably generous gesture. Men like Adrian represent the best of the rugby community.

The GAA community were quick to rally too. They allowed us to hold a bucket collection outside Pearse Stadium, the home of Galway GAA, before the County Hurling Championship Final of 2019.

Since my accident and paralysis I have severely reduced proprioception, which is the body's ability to know where it is in space with a sense of its position, location, orientation and movement. It's usually present in every muscle movement we have. Proprioception comes from the sensory receptors in skin, the inner ear, muscles, joints and tendons. When you move, these receptors send messages to your brain about your positions and actions. Your brain then processes these messages and works with your vision, nervous system and vestibular (balance and co-ordination) system to create your perception of where your body is and how you're moving. It's proprioception that allows you to walk without consciously thinking about where you are going to place your foot next. It enables you to balance on one leg, to touch your elbow or your nose with your eyes closed, and tells your body that you have moved from walking on grass to a cement path. However, without proprioception, I can't move without thinking about my next step, or where I need to position my body so I won't fall over.

As I trained to improve both my walking and my balance, that lack of proprioception constantly put obstacles in my way. One summer's day, when I was still doing things with Mandy and the kids, we went to Strandhill in Sligo, a beautiful place. We had driven up separately, but it was great to be even on the same beach with them. Walking on loose sand is very tricky for me, and it was more difficult back then. It was a struggle to get myself up and down off the sand as there's nothing to pull yourself up on in the middle of the beach. I was just flopping myself down on the sand. But I managed to make my way to the far end of the beach, where Mandy and the kids were. But then I went into the sea, to enjoy the Atlantic water. I went into the water and it was really hard as I edged my way in because I was losing even more sensation as the water came up over my legs. You can walk out a good bit in Strandhill before it gets deep, but when it got up to about my knees I started to lose my balance. That movement of the water kept on knocking me over. As I tried to get back in, the tiniest little waves were knocking me over. That's how weak I was on my feet and how unsure I was.

Things went from bad to worse at home. In August I got two St Bernard dogs. I said they were for Bradley and Aimee but I really got them for company for myself as I felt so lonely. There's nothing more lonely than being in a place with somebody when there's complete silence. I found that extremely hard. And then, how stupid was I? I went back to talking online at night because I couldn't sleep. There's no excuse, and it was my own fault. Mandy found out, of course. She knew I couldn't have been meeting anyone, but that was the end for her.

Mandy and I are very different, but we built a good life together, and have three wonderful children. All I ever wanted was to build a better life for my family. I know now I didn't always go about it the right way, that I put business first. But I am still surprised at how quickly it all fell apart, and how we both crossed lines that we could never have imagined and could never step back over. Maybe that's what always happens when marriages and relationships break down.

At the end of August it was clear that our marriage was over.

It was a terrible time. My head was still in a mess and the medications weren't helping. I was still on antidepressants, and the OxyNorm was really messing with my head. I wasn't violent, but my mood swings were volatile, veering from sadness to despair to irritability to anger. I moved back in with my parents. Thankfully I could do that, otherwise I would have been homeless.

Divorce is very difficult for anyone, but like many men I found it was additionally difficult having to rebuild my life with nothing. The business was still operating, but it was failing. I had to have a place to stay for the kids, but I couldn't take any money from the business because there was none in it – everything was maxed out.

I was dealing with all the debts from the business, including both our cars.

Someone told me to go up to the local Intreo office, that there were supports I could get. I had never ever asked for a handout from the State in my life, but I went up. I was still obviously disabled when I went in and said, 'I need help.' There was no compassion, no understanding of the severity of my situation. I was just given forms to fill out. I left completely disillusioned and dejected, in tears.

After a few months I did secure an invalidity pension, but when I looked for help with housing I was told I was over the threshold limit. There was a payment for a bus I had sold in my account and I didn't have it documented right so they counted that as income, rather than the sale of an asset. That put me just above the income threshold. To manage financially, to pay off debts and car payments, I had been selling tools and other bits that I had in the yard. I just gave up.

September was a bad month. I didn't get to see the kids at all and I also injured my ankle. I couldn't remember how it happened because I have no sensation. I could have gone over on it at any stage. I may have just bent it on a step, causing it to flare up. It was bruised and swollen, but I didn't feel the pain. Because I have poor circulation and no feeling my healing process is a lot slower, so for two weeks it really curtailed my training, and in those two weeks I was worried that the challenge was over before it had begun. Luckily I was able to start training again, building up my stamina and the distance I could walk.

Despite everything, we finally got to the starting line of the Toughest Trek, and we had a big launch. It began in my yard, right beside where the accident happened, and Galway Bay FM and photographers came out. There were over 120 people there who were going to do the first stage of the walk to Craughwell village, about five or six kilometres. Derek Carroll and Pete Burke were coming the full distance with me.

The longest distance I had probably walked in any one day was 20 or 25km. Now we had to walk an average of 42km a day, for five days!

I was walking very slowly – but fast for me – and when we got to Craughwell we stopped at Jody's service station, which was owned by Derek's father-in-law. There were teas and coffees for people, and some more photo shoots. That's where the vast majority of people left, though a mate named Martin Brady who I had been in school with decided he would keep going, even though he was wearing chinos, and a pair of smart shoes that weren't suitable for walking any distance. He did manage to walk those first 48 kilometres with us, which was tough going – even some strong Athenry hurlers weren't able to complete it – but I don't think he'd volunteer again! Pete had arranged for a group of people from Ability West to join me on the walk. They alone raised €5,000 for us, even though they are a charitable organisation themselves, one that looks after people with physical and mental disabilities. I thought they were just brilliant. To this day, I include them as one of the groups I raise funds for.

My mother came along in the car, as she was a bit frail. She has a lot of health challenges and issues. A truck reversed over her leg a long time ago, and she spent weeks in hospital. They saved the leg, but she has never been right since. The last five or six years of my life have definitely taken a toll on her. However, Dad joined us for part of the walk, despite his bad hips, and he had a pint in a pub along the way when he hopped into the support car. We stopped in Aughrim, at about the 35km mark, and I was just shattered, but the old fella went off and found another pub!

Getting from one side of Ballinasloe to the other took me nearly an hour because I was so weak. Someone would have to hold my hand so I could lift my leg just to get up on the kerb. The Shearwater Hotel in Ballinasloe had sponsored rooms for the few of us continuing the walk, and a bus was organised to bring everyone else back to Athenry. Now I was absolutely flaked, and I just wanted to get something to eat and go to bed, but I could see that the bus wasn't moving off. They were waiting for Dad, who had found another barstool, and I had to tell him to get on the bus so they could all go home. I think he was so proud of what was happening that he wanted to enjoy the moment and tell everyone he met about it.

We were all exhausted, everyone had found it tough, but that night in Ballinasloe I genuinely didn't think I would be able to walk the next day. I continuously had to put my hand on someone for support because my legs were so weak. It was hard to know what was going on because I had no sensation. I did everything I could think of – cold baths, rest – but my legs were bouncing off the bed with spasms all night.

The next morning we were all in bits, even Derek and Pete, who are fully abled, but new people joined us and that pushed us on. When you want something bad enough, it keeps you going forward. We got moving again, and that night we knew we would be able to get up and go on the following morning, regardless of how we felt.

It took us five days to walk across the country, and it was an amazing experience. As I walked I was talking to friends, people who really wanted to be there with me, people who knew what it meant to me. Different people met us along the route; some joined us for hours, others for a few days. Paul Neary, my best mate from school, who lives in Belfast, joined me whenever he could.

It was heart-warming.

I was so determined to do every inch that when I had to get the support car to take me to a toilet, on the road between Kilcock and Enfield, I insisted that we didn't wait until the others caught up. I made the driver, my aunt Breda Farrell, turn around and take me back to the exact spot I had got into the car. I was not going to miss a step.

On the last day, we came into Dublin. I found walking along the Grand Canal one of the longest stretches. When we turned off onto Leeson Street we felt that we were close, but there was still a long way to go, and a lot of it was uphill. As we slogged along the last few kilometres there was a crowd shouting and waving banners on the flyover bridge at Foxrock Church, cheering us on. I started to get emotional. Only a few kilometres to go. One of my friends from the NRH came and joined me for the last bit in his wheelchair, and when we passed the house of another friend who'd been a patient with us, he was out as well. We passed by Bakers' Corner, where we had had some great nights together.

On the night of 26 October 2019 I walked back through the doors of the NRH, to a great reception. I had a badly injured foot and I was exhausted, but I had done it. How did I do it? It was because of people: my friends, and the health professionals who had supported me. All the solid relationships I had given time to during my life were there for me. Not the fickle and contractual relationships I've made through business or along the way, but the real relationships. My friends and family had come together for me. It was one of the best feelings I ever had, even though I was completely worn out and sore.

To this day, it's the biggest success I've had, in terms of perseverance, and succeeding at a challenge I had set myself. Hearing the applause that night was a great moment. I understood that this was what life was about, all the good bits anyway: enjoying the moment, friendships, relationships, sacrifice, challenge, doing your best, and trying to be a good person. Even now when I think about the moment walking through those doors, and all it represented, I still get overwhelmed.

The feeling after finishing those 206 kilometres was phenomenal, but it is no lie to say that my feet were in shreds. There was no skin left on the ball of one foot and two of the toes. That was from a blister that had burst on day two, and then it had rained on day three and my foot had got wet. Éimear Smith – who had advised me not to walk, for my own sake – was among the crowd there to welcome and congratulate me, and because I was still officially her patient, she took me up and looked after my feet. The damage was so bad that, even though I cannot feel anything, it had gone so deep that there was some kind of awareness, some sensation of something new going on. I had started to feel a tingle, and my legs and feet were twitching like mad. When I took off my sock and saw what it looked like I said, 'Sometimes it's great not to have feelings!'

It took about two months to heal, I was treating my feet every night and wrapping them up in bandages. But it was well worth it. We raised around €65,000 for the NRH to be used for its Physiotherapy and Spinal Outreach Programmes.

The walk had given me back a purpose. It was hard, but I completed it. I achieved all my aims: to raise money for the NRH; to help me reset my own mindset; to celebrate my anniversary; and to show my gratitude to all the people who had helped me along the way since my accident, by showing them how far I had come. It also symbolised to me the coming together of all the people who had supported me and the cause. I realised what a great bunch of people I had around me, and in my corner, and that brought home once again the need to make time for relationships and for friends.

It was making relationships that had saved me in the first place. If I hadn't taken time to get to know Ger Brady back in the day, he would have driven past me near that bridge. He wouldn't have recognised me and stopped me doing a terrible thing. Everything since the accident was teaching me the importance of relationships, relationships I had lost when I became a ratty short-fused business person who thought he was too good for everybody. That wasn't me, but that was what society was telling me I needed to be to succeed, and that is why I had been so sad and upset. I wasn't the person I should have been. I realised I wasn't just rebuilding relationships any more. I was rebuilding myself.

THE ROAD TO SUCCESS IS NEVER SMOOTH.

My journey to rebuild myself as a man has been filled with many victories, but it has also been littered with failures, and mistakes, and regrets, and challenge after challenge. However, the feeling of achieving something that you have worked hard for, and overcome obstacles for, and persevered through pain for, is hard to top.

17

THE JOY OF PEEING

After the accident I had to be catheterised. The nurses would take away the bags of urine and plug fresh empty ones back in.

I had been in St Finbar's in Galway a couple of weeks when a nurse, I think she was a specialist, sat down beside the bed and started talking to me. She showed me a catheter bag, a tube and a little leaflet to read. She told me she had heard that I was getting movement in my toe, and now could be a good time to start thinking about self-catheterisation.

At that time I wasn't even getting my head around the pain, and my disability, and not being able to walk. My business was already beginning to tank because I wasn't there, and Trafalgar had cancelled our contract. My head just wasn't in the place to even contemplate sticking a tube up my own penis and into my bladder. I had enough going on. I couldn't think of anything more horrific at that moment, and I got very overwhelmed at the idea of it, and told her to leave me alone, and she did. I didn't have the headspace for something else.

But when I got to the NRH, the realisation finally came that rehabilitation meant doing things for myself, and the more I did the better I was going to be. So when self-catheterisation was suggested to me again, I got my head around it. They explain to you how you do it, you get the tube ready to insert, you hold on to it, pull back your foreskin and just go for it. They sent me off to try it, and that first time I pulled the curtains around my cubicle and lay on the bed. Even now the thought of that tube slipping up inside is horrific. But, my bladder was bursting so I filled the bag. And after that it got easier, and easier, until I could nearly do it blindfolded whenever I needed to empty my bladder. It was another step towards gaining my independence.

I still had regular accidents, and just before I left the NRH I did some tests and the urologist told me I had very little pressure or strength in my bladder, so I would be self-catheterising for at least another year. That nearly destroyed me, because as good as it was to not have a bag hanging around my leg the whole time, self-catheterisation meant bringing these big pouches around everywhere with me and planning everything around both my bowels and my bladder. I hated it. It was so debilitating.

I was in a foul humour when I left that appointment to go to my physio session. Sorcha could see that I was fed up and asked me what was going on. I told her I was upset that the urologist had just said he would see me next year. Sorcha, as always, knew how to get me back on track. She told me about a person who had cancer that affected his bladder, and he had to retrain it. She reminded me that I had been working hard to get back on my feet, and that my bladder was just another muscle that could be retrained. She suggested that I use the tools I had used until now – hard work and visualisation.

She gave me the confidence that I could succeed. And from that moment, whenever I needed to self-catheterise to empty my bladder I would go into the toilet and I would stand up as if I was peeing. I did that over and over again, visualising myself feeling the pressure and peeing every time I emptied my bladder. I was still catheterising but I always made sure to turn on the tap, stand over a toilet or urinal, listen to the running water, and before inserting the tube wait to see if I could pee on my own first. I did this hundreds and hundreds of times, but nothing ever happened.

Weeks later, on 18 May, when I was crashing mentally, I drove myself to Limerick for that stag party, but first I met up with Joe Noone. We were in a pub watching Munster vs Leinster and chatting away.

I was trying to push all the bad stuff going on in my head, that I had lost the will to live, to the back of my mind, so it just shows you how good we can all be at hiding stuff. I had a couple of pints and I went to the toilet with my bag of stuff. As usual, I did the same visualisation, but this time the pee started to trickle out of me. It was a wonderful feeling. That sensation of being able to pee for the first time in months was insane. It was one of the most beautiful moments in my recovery, because it was a huge part of getting my independence back again. So it trickled away, and I was able to empty it to a certain degree, but I still catheterised to make sure it was empty.

I cannot put into words how exhilarating the feeling of urinating is when you'd previously thought it might never happen again. We have all been peeing from a few hours old, it's just a basic bodily function. So, unless you have experienced it, it's impossible to explain what it's like not to have the function to be able to pee at will any more, and then to regain it. I rank that moment up there with the euphoria of moving my big toe and of walking out the doors of the NRH. It was a huge accomplishment, another important cornerstone completed.

I went out to Joe and I had the biggest smile on my face, and I told him, 'I'm after fucking peeing! I'm after peeing!' I know Joe was delighted for me, but he couldn't understand my elation. That satisfaction of being able to go for a pee was exhilarating.

From there, I never looked back, though it wasn't simple. I couldn't just think about going to the toilet and go. I might be there for five minutes before it came out, but it eventually would.

There was one downside. I got a lot of bad bladder and urinary tract infections, and I still get them. I can have one for a while and not realise, because of my lack of sensation. So when I do finally feel the pain it means I've got to stage two and I need to go into hospital and get intravenous antibiotics to stop the infection spreading any further.

But that doesn't take away from that deliriously happy moment in my life, standing over a urinal in a Limerick City bar and the joy of peeing.

VISUALISE.

I have used visualisation constantly since my accident to help me reach the milestones and improvements and successes I want. I don't like using the word dreams, so set your targets or your goals and picture yourself achieving them. However, don't think you will get there without working hard.

18

COVID AND COLD WATER

I eventually moved out from my parents' house in December 2019 and began renting a house locally. It was big and cold, but it was the first time I had lived independently since the accident. I couldn't afford the rent so two other lads who used to work for me, Pat Flannery and Ian Raftery, moved in. They were great to share a house with. We eventually had to move out when the house owners got planning permission. I moved back with my parents, and that's when I converted part of their property into my own apartment, with bedrooms for the kids to stay, and this is where I still live. I furnished the whole lot, including a kitchen, for €2,600, picking up everything, bit by bit, on Facebook Marketplace.

After the walk I had started looking for other challenges, or ways to occupy my mind, and in February 2020 we ran a fundraising Valentine's Ball. Rugby legend Jamie Heaslip came and spoke at that. Helping to organise the event kept my brain busy and my mind off the pain and my debts. It was my way of coping.

Damo had also just asked me to be part of Project Empower, a row across the Atlantic from New York to Galway, and I was really excited about the prospect, and the training that lay ahead. I was in flying form, and before Christmas I had decided I was going to start dating again. Maybe I was looking for another kind of distraction, but I also missed affection, and I didn't want to be alone. Loneliness is something I genuinely fear. And I did meet a woman online, from Spain, and she came to Ireland, and I went to see her in Madrid.

I really liked her; she was a sound girl. She came to the Valentine's Ball and we had a fabulous weekend. At one stage we disappeared up into the hotel room and everyone thought we were up to something, but she was actually helping me count out the money for Jamie Heaslip's fee, which he never took! I still owe him a huge debt of gratitude. His kindness meant we made money for the charity.

We stayed in contact and talked every day, and one Friday in mid-March 2020 I was in Madrid when it was announced that the country would shut down at midnight, and everyone had to stay indoors, to stop the spread of COVID-19. We had spent the day looking around the royal palace in Madrid and took pictures on the Gran Vía – she lived just off it – which was really busy. We had a few beers and stocked up with groceries and we prepared to stay in the apartment. I was due to fly out two days later so I hadn't a clue what was going to happen.

We didn't budge from the apartment the next day. I was still slipping a lot at the time and even though the apartment was tiny somehow I managed to slip and take a chunk out of the side of my foot. But in Madrid the pharmacies ran a delivery service. They sent supplies to fix me up.

I was due to fly out on the Sunday, but while I waited to hear what was happening we slipped out and took a picture on the deserted Gran Via. Eventually I was told to get to the airport hotel and to stay isolated in a room until I got further word. I stayed

Monivea RFC underage blitz, 1989. I'm in the back row, second from the left.

Only 17 years of age and one of the proudest moments in my life: getting to wear the green of Ireland.

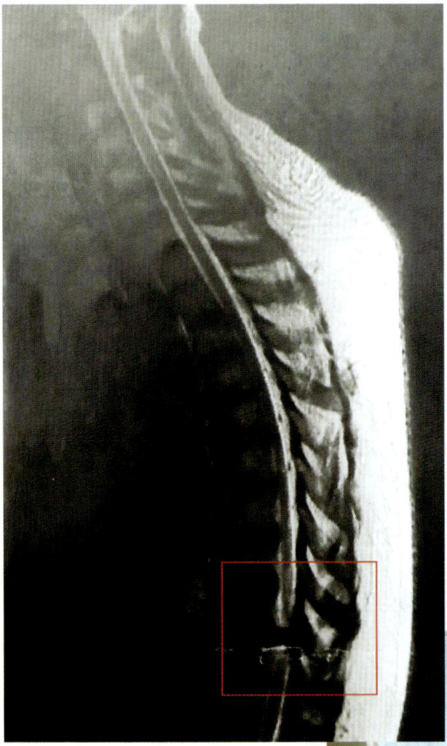

An MRI of the spinal cord that was almost completely severed and the ruptured disc that changed my life for ever.

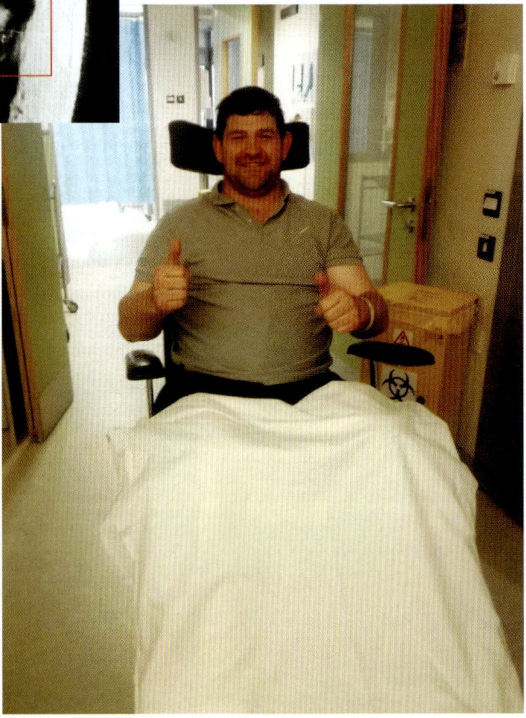

One of my first days in one of the specially designed wheelchairs in the Mater. I had to be hoisted by a machine from the bed into the wheelchair. As you can see, I was being as positive as possible. But behind it all, I was crumbling.

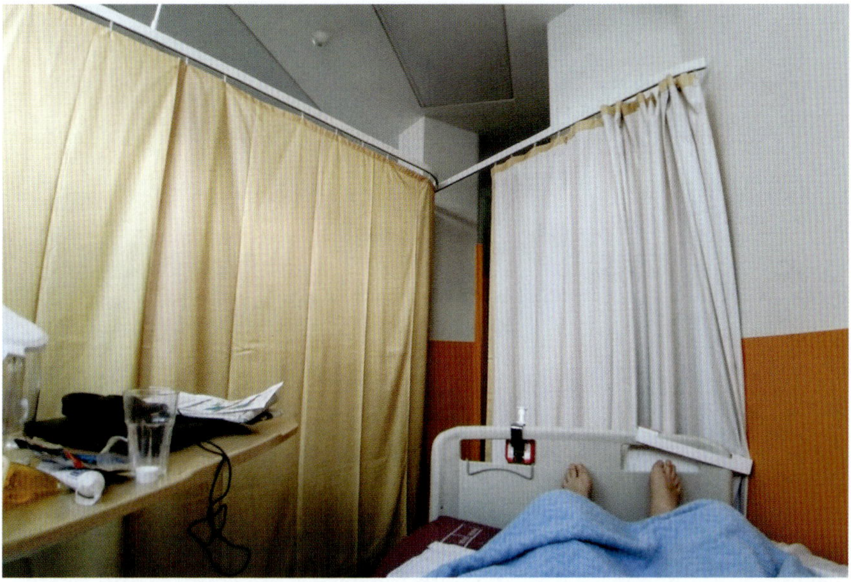

Early days at the National Rehabilitation Hospital.

Playing wheelchair basketball.

The Toughest Trek. What an amazing moment in my life. The joy of seeing so many people walking with me across the country and raising €65,000 for the NRH was only possible because of incredible help from friends and family. (© Mike Shaughnessy)

Training was tough going in preparation for the upcoming challenge of rowing from New York to Galway. My pet dogs Sniffy and Meduas were always by my side. (© Emilija Jefremova)

A short training day in our rowing boat *Cushlamachree* on Galway Bay with the boat builder, Justin Adkin, before it was shipped to New York. (© Emilija Jefremova)

One of the most magical and long-lasting memories I have from the challenge is rowing around the Statue of Liberty while training. What an awesome experience. (© Emilija Jefremova)

Emilija capturing a moment during a photoshoot which probably illustrates the anxiety and lack of sleep I was experiencing the best. (© Emilija Jefremova)

I was so thrilled for Damo for completing the challenge of rowing from New York to Galway and was delighted to be greeting him on the docks. However, the sense of failure was crippling me; destroying me internally. (© Emilija Jefremova)

It's just a simple wall, but how lucky I am that, in February 2025, I was able to build it. I had the time and physical capabilities to do so. So many people don't have one or the other. I'm so lucky to have both. Years ago I had the physical capabilities but not the time. I believe time is our greatest commodity. Make the most of it.

Life is beautiful and surprising. Who would have guessed that after my accident I would become a keynote and public speaker for companies, organisations and charities? I love sharing my story and my learnings since 2018 and seeing the long-lasting impact they have on people.

My three wonderful kids are the most important thing in my life. I love sharing experiences with them, like this time in Paris at the Eiffel Tower in November 2022. I'm hoping they develop the same love of travelling as I have.

My family: the people who are closest and dearest to me in one picture. My parents' fiftieth wedding anniversary in August 2024. A simple but lovely celebration.

there for two days before getting a flight home. The airport was practically deserted and everyone seemed scared and nervous, and when I finally got on board there were only five or six other people on the flight.

We stayed in touch for a while, but lost contact during COVID. It had been a great distraction from my condition. I had really enjoyed spending time with her, and going off and seeing new places, and meeting new people, being somewhere different.

Before my accident I wasn't open to anything that I saw as 'alternative'. I had a closed mind. However, during my recovery I tried a lot of new things to help me cope. I wasn't afraid. What harm could they do? I tried hot yoga. I did Pilates for a while. I tried acupuncture, which was brilliant, once I found the right practitioner. I was also blown away by my response to reflexology. I don't know whether it helped me with recovery, but I just loved the sensations it triggered. I couldn't feel what the therapist was doing at my feet, but I could feel these new sensations run through my body and up into my neck. That told me there was a connection somewhere, even though I was not feeling anything it was telling my brain that there was a connection. I found that fascinating.

However, what really helped with the pain, and I didn't realise it would at the time, was the Freezebury challenge. Damo encouraged me to do it as part of our preparations for Project Empower. He and Johnny O'Connor had come up with the idea of Freezebury the previous year. They were winter sea bathers and had wondered if it would be possible to swim in the Atlantic every day of what is historically the coldest month for west coast of Ireland sea temperatures, adding a minute each day.

On the first day of the Freezebury challenge you go into the ocean, the cold water, for one minute, and the second day you spend two minutes in the water, and so on until 28 February – or 29 February that year because it was a leap year, when you stay in for 29 minutes. The rules were shorts, speedos, swimsuits or bikinis only – no wetsuits, hats, gloves, booties, trainers or rash vests. You had to be submerged to your upper chest for the duration and submerge your head fully at least once.

On 1 February, Damo and I went into the sea near the diving board on Salthill Promenade. I walked in rather than jumping because I had no idea how I would react. I ducked my head under for a few seconds, and experienced an immediate brain freeze. Because of my lack of proprioception the tide and the water messed with my balance, and fair play to Damo, he understood that immediately. When he saw me struggling to get back out, he put out his hands so I could hold on to him as I got out of the water. We dried off, put on our clothes, hopped into the car, and cranked up the heater. But when we walked into a restaurant to grab some coffees we were still freezing.

I did a few days of cold water immersion with Damo and then did my own thing, going in for longer every day. It was hard, but I was about trying everything and anything I could. The one advantage of having a lack of feeling in my feet and legs was that I didn't feel the cold until the water was up past my waist. I'd look very brave, unflinching in the cold water, while everyone else was struggling, but once it hit above my waist I would feel the cold kick in. However, I also couldn't feel the stones or rocks under my feet, so I cut them very easily.

I went into the water a lot in Blackrock and Salthill, but I also went out to Renvyle, to a park past Oranmore where there is a little marina, and into Loughrea Lake. I drove out to Dog's Bay in Connemara, beside Roundstone, and out to what I think of as my grandmother's beach in Carna. I went into the water there just to evoke memories for myself of good times when I was a child.

I did most of those cold water immersions on my own. I brought my kids to Salthill one night and they stood there and watched me as I swam around before clambering out. It was freezing, and they were laughing at me, but they came with me a few more times to give me support. I was very committed to it. Going into water at night is a very cool experience, but I wouldn't go anywhere near the sea if it was wild, though strangely, the water can feel colder when it is calmer.

The brain freeze after putting your head under water isn't a comfortable feeling, and it can take for ever to warm up. It would be at the very least a half-hour drive home, usually more, and I'd be shivering the entire time, even with the seat warmers on and the heater up full blast. But it was so enjoyable, I actually began to look forward to the sensation afterwards.

And when I finished that month of cold water immersion I felt different, both physically and mentally. I felt so much better in myself. When I started doing it my nerve pain was through the roof, no matter what I was taking. I couldn't switch it off. However, a few days after it ended I noted my nerve pain was way down, from about 100 per cent to 60 per cent, a massive reduction. Prior to this it might have reduced occasionally, but never for more than a few hours, certainly never days. Then another few days passed and it was still down, and it stayed down. It was a huge win.

I have no idea why. Maybe it was something else, but submerging myself in cold water coincided with that massive reduction in pain. I have my own theory. If you put a bag of defrosted peas in the freezer and take it out an hour later the outside of the bag will be frozen, but the inside will still be soft. And I thought of my body like that. My injury was a spinal cord injury, right in the middle of my body surrounded by fat and muscles, and there was swelling in there from the injury. In my opinion, just being in the water for that period of time gave it time for the coldness to get into your body, and to help reduce the swelling, which took the pressure off the spinal cord. It's not science, but it's how I picture what happened.

So that was a huge win for me, and an unexpected one. The pain has never increased since then. I've done a week or two of immersion in the ocean again, but it has never decreased any further, so I think that's the level it's going to stay at. I still occasionally submerge myself in the ocean, and I only ever take cold showers.

Now if I go a few days without a cold shower, I feel off. Cold water is a godsend for me, because when I'm thinking about the cold, and about getting myself clean as quickly as possible, I'm not thinking about the pain. I love the sensation when you emerge from the cold water. If I lived near the sea I would swim every day, but a shower is a good alternative.

We launched Project Empower just before the first COVID lockdown. Immediately our plans for training and meetings had to be adapted and changed, and eventually we would have to postpone the row. However, I think I found COVID easier than a lot of people did. I was used to being alone, being isolated. Even at the NRH, where I was surrounded by other people, I was still away from friends and family.

It might sound strange, but I enjoyed many of the restrictions the pandemic brought, because it was downtime, and not being able to go too far was okay for me. I found I was beginning to appreciate the small things around me, to appreciate and to be able to enjoy time. Because nothing could be done I found it peaceful, and it allowed me to spend more time with my kids, which was brilliant. The pandemic also got me outdoors more, and corny though it may sound I found that reconnecting with nature brought me a new outlook and excitement. I would bring the kids out to this really tiny beach that we'd discovered, out by Tullycross, and it reminded me how much I love Connemara.

So one lovely day I decided I would go back out to Connemara and try one of the easier trails up Diamond Hill in Connemara National Park. I had been to Diamond Hill so many times with busloads but I was a big lazy fucker and I was too busy making phone calls or doing business that I never made the time to climb it myself. I was on my own when I stood at the bottom of Diamond Hill and began putting one foot in front of the other. I was on my own because I didn't want to have someone with me and fail. If I was going to fall, if I was going to fail, I would do it on my own. Because of my lack of proprioception I had to keep my eyes on my feet, on the ground, all the time to see where each foot was going to land, and to adjust my body so I wouldn't fall. If I gauged it wrong and my foot was skewed when it landed I would slip and possibly take a tumble. I needed to have my body braced for each different impact. My brain has to process very quickly what I see in front of me, so climbing steeper, varied terrain was obviously far more difficult than walking along a flat path. There weren't two steps the same, which is exhausting for me.

But I did it. It was tough going, but I made it to the top. I took a video of myself, sweating and out of breath but ecstatic. No gym could replicate this for the body. It was such a buzz. I felt that moments like that were what living life is all about. I posted that video on @the_toughest_trek to show people that if they really wanted to do something it could be in their grasp. It was one of the most empowering videos I did for myself. I had conquered something again. It was another step in my recovery, another landmark moment. It took me 41 years to get up on top of that hill, which was silly, but I'm glad I finally made it. Coming down was actually the hardest part. I slipped a few times, but I was grand.

In October 2020 I had to go into hospital to get my gallbladder removed. Spending a week in there without seeing anybody was tough and I don't know how I lasted. I had come to loathe hospitals. It wasn't because of the people, or the services, but because you were there for a reason, and it wasn't ever a good one. The gallbladder had been at me for a very long time, from before the accident, but I hadn't realised that's what had been causing me so much pain. I had a severe attack in the NRH, but with all that was happening they didn't realise what it was. When I was getting regular attacks they investigated further and it turned out I had a rare condition where large gallstones kept on getting stuck on top of the duct. They couldn't get rid of my gallstones; the gallbladder had to go completely. However, they didn't want to take it out because the gallbladder acts as a digestive filter and I already had digestive and bowel issues. But months after I left the NRH I started having regular crippling attacks. I was well able to put up with a lot of pain at this stage, but this particular pain was flooring me. An attack could go on for hours and hours and the only way to relieve it was a morphine drip. I discovered that they couldn't give that to you if you arrived into casualty, but they could give it to you if you called out the ambulance, so that's what I used to do. The minute they put the morphine into me I'd start getting relief.

I went into A&E one time on my own during COVID, and they wouldn't give me any pain relief. I was in a state, bent over roaring and begging for something. I told the nurse, a woman I knew, what drugs I was on. I told her I was on oxy, but none of it was working. I needed IV morphine. But she wouldn't listen. Instead she told me, 'When you act like a grownup, I'll treat you like a grownup.' That was a tough moment. There was just no talking to her and I was so angry and distraught I got up, ripped out the cannula, and walked out of the hospital. The pain had finally begun to reduce a little and I walked into Galway city, which was deserted. I needed to go to the toilet – I still hadn't full control of my bowels or bladder at this stage – but there was nowhere to go, as everywhere had been closed because of the pandemic. There was nobody around. I was just miserable, and crying my eyes out, and I started walking out towards home, inching my way along the motorway in the early hours of the morning.

My parents were trying to reach me, but I wouldn't even answer my phone. My mind had gone haywire again. They were worried about me – it wasn't long after I had been in the psychiatric ward – but eventually I must have answered because Dad came and picked me up at the side of the motorway. That must have been such a very worrying time for my parents; they were obviously terrified that I was suicidal again, but I wasn't. I was just miserable because of the pain, and at that point had given up caring. Within a few days I had another episode, and this time I called the ambulance. I was back in casualty again, and when I was put through to a consultant I told them, 'I need this out'. They agreed to do it and within a few days I was admitted for the operation.

I was there for about a week. They had to clear an infection before they could operate. I was away from the kids, and there with no one to talk to, no one I even felt I could chat on the phone to. I was feeling emotionally isolated, and desperately lonely, and it all started gnawing away again at my head. It was an extremely difficult time for me, and not a time I like reflecting back on, because once again, my mental state was just not in a good place.

Instagram, October 2020

One thing that drives me cracked about social media is that people only portray their good and happy side. There is nothing as such wrong with it, once you are not afraid to show that you are fragile, hurt or sad at times. I've endured a couple of hard weeks in and out of hospital etc. I admit it got me down and made me think negatively at times. However I kept saying to myself life always has its up and downs but we live for the good

> times. Always remember no matter how dark times can get, they only make your good times feel even greater.

But once I got out of hospital I was in a better place mentally. In hospital, I think I had just dived back down into 'poor me' syndrome' and couldn't dig myself out. Now, I felt I was ready to start building myself up again. I had Project Empower ahead of me. I knew that was something to work towards, and continuing that training programme would help me both physically and mentally.

STEP OUT OF YOUR COMFORT ZONE. YOU NEVER KNOW WHERE IT WILL TAKE YOU.

Since my accident I have realised that opening up my mind to trying new things, and taking challenges that bring me further out of my comfort zone, can bring unexpected joys and outcomes. There are unexpected wins around every corner.

19

PROJECT EMPOWER

HOW TO ROW ACROSS AN OCEAN

One thing that really got to me after my accident was feeling that people were looking at me with pity rather than respect. I'm sure people didn't mean it badly, but there were times after I was back on my feet when someone offered me something free, or even gave me an envelope of money – which I would put straight into the fund for the NRH – and it made me feel awful. I wasn't looking for pity. I was able to support myself, even if it was a struggle. It just felt so demeaning.

That probably wasn't what people intended; I'm sure they meant well, but that's where my mind was at. Having people pity me, rather than respect me, hurt me. But I wouldn't say anything. I would just talk with my feet and leave a situation or avoid someone. Pride definitely got in my way at times. Maybe when I thought people were looking at me with pity it was because I was looking at myself with pity. Whatever the reasons, that's where my mindset was for a long time, and once again OxyNorm probably played its part in how I viewed the world. So when Damo offered me another opportunity to do something that could restore my pride, earn me respect, I jumped at it.

Damo and I had become firm friends through rugby. We had played against each other as youngsters, so it started out as a bit of competitive aggression towards one another. We ended up playing together for Connacht underage, and then when I moved to Galwegians we were the two youngest in the squad and became great buddies. We also went to South Africa together to train, with Niall O'Brien, Phelim Cloonan, John Gavin and Joe Noone. Damo went on to have a professional rugby career, and when he hung up his boots he began taking on some incredible challenges and extreme adventures, including the Marathon des Sables, a seven-day ultramarathon in the Sahara, and a 63-day solo row across the Atlantic from the Canary Islands to Antigua. He constantly tested and pushed himself.

We had enjoyed an adventure together already. I had always said to Mandy, and she agreed, that if I ever got the opportunity to see mountain gorillas in the wild I would take that opportunity. So fair play to her, when Damo told me he was going on a trip to Rwanda and the Congo to climb a volcano in the Nyiragongo National Park and see the gorillas she let me off. I was in my early thirties, just after a hip resurfacing, was overweight, unfit, ill-equipped, and had never climbed a mountain. However, I made it, despite my unsuitable boots falling apart, and got to spend a night above a lava lake in the middle of a storm, and, even more memorably, 40 incredible awe-filled minutes silently watching a group of gorillas in the forest.

Damo had joined me on the Toughest Trek for two separate days the previous October and had seen how difficult that was for me. I still had very short steps and it was a massive struggle, but he had seen my determination. I, meanwhile, had begun to understand why Damo does what he does, why he is so driven.

He had told me about a plan to row from New York to Ireland with his brother Andrew, and I remember saying to him, 'I'd love to do that!' Then, shortly after the walk, when we were having a bite to eat at the Huntsman in Galway, he said, 'Gussy, I want to ask you something. Do you want to come on the row with me?' His brother's partner was expecting a baby and he didn't want to miss the birth. I didn't hesitate for a second. 'Yes, a hundred per cent!' I didn't think about whether I could do it or not. He had put a challenge in front of me. I was in!

Far more people reach the summit of Mount Everest every year than have rowed the North Atlantic Ocean. Our goal was, in June 2021, to row, unsupported, approximately 5,000km from New York across the North Atlantic to Galway city – and to row it in record time. The record of 55 days and 13 hours had been set in 1896 by Norwegians George Harbo and Frank Samuelsen. They were the first on record to row across the Atlantic, from New York to the Scilly Isles. Eleven pairs of rowers had failed to better that record; five never completed the crossings.

After my cross-country walk I thought I was physically fit. So as soon as I left Damo I headed to the District Gym and got on the rowing machine. I only lasted five minutes! That wasn't going to get us far. Time to put my head down and put in some hard work.

My aim for Project Empower was to inspire others, to increase awareness of spinal cord injuries, and to raise money for charities: I chose ones close to my heart, the NRH and Ability West. Damo chose Madra Dog Rescue and Macdara chose Galway Simon Community.

I also viewed it as a way to keep the head straight. I knew if I had a big challenge in front of me that would keep me focused on my physical improvements and give me a purpose to keep fighting. I wanted to show what you can achieve by hard work, determination and never giving up on yourself.

Because Damo had rowed an ocean before he knew the ins and outs. He estimated that it was going to cost about €150,000. The boat alone would be £70,000 sterling. It was made clear from the start that Project Empower was his project, and that he would own all the rights, the social media, the boat. That felt fair to me; it was his idea, after all, and he had the experience. However, I did think I would be seen as a partner in other ways.

He brought in a project manager, MacDara Hosty, to raise money and sponsorship for the project. Things were going along nicely and we were having regular meetings, but then COVID came and we went on to Zoom. And eventually it was decided to postpone it for a year, to June 2022, but that we would keep training and fundraising.

For the launch of Project Empower, to publicise our plan, it was decided we would row, traditional style, from Inisheer in the Aran Islands into Galway city, about 42km. So in August 2020 Padraig Folan from Carraroe showed us how to row a currach, which is so much harder than it looks. It was my first time rowing in the open sea.

I met the photographer Emilija Jefremova for the first time in Carraroe. She would become a regular companion to us along the way, and it was Emilija who photographed me for this book's cover. She would also become part of the crew when Tomek Ciezki, from Heavy Man Films, decided to do a documentary about our endeavours. They were always great to be around, and never intrusive.

I loved learning from Padraig, even though it is such a difficult craft to master, and Damo and I got very frustrated with each other. The two of us had to have our stroke exactly the same, of equal power, otherwise the boat went all over the place. After those sessions I had a totally different understanding of the skills it takes to row those boats, and the people who row them.

Traditional currachs don't have a rudder, but we didn't have enough time to master our rowing before the October launch, and Padraig knew we would never manage the full distance without one. We would need one if we were to keep ourselves on track and steer ourselves into Galway harbour.

We got the ferry out to Inisheer the night before to stay in the hotel and had a great bit of craic with everyone. We planned to start around six o'clock in the morning when it was still dark, and Emilija got some lovely photographs. However, it wasn't as straightforward as we had expected. We had always launched from a pier, where you just step into the currach, but this time we were launching from the beach, and had to push the boat out and jump into it. That was something new that my body hadn't learned, hadn't mastered, and the water messed with my balance. I struggled, but we eventually managed it, despite a wave nearly turning us over and throwing us both back out again. However, at some stage during the launch I lost one of my runners. I had to row with my bare foot against a wooden strut which caused a deep cut into the flesh. By the end my foot was badly damaged and bleeding. This would have been excruciating for someone with sensation in their lower limbs, and I was even beginning to feel something!

It was tough. We were bailing water out at stages, and when we arrived at the docks almost nine hours later we were cold and exhausted. It was a wonderful feeling to have made it, but there was no time for celebration. Our friend Shorty, Christian Short, was there to meet us and I just had time to change quickly before rushing off to pick up the kids.

Luckily our ocean vessel would not be a currach, but the *Cushlamachree*, a 6.2m SeaSabre handmade by Justin Adkin in Devon, England. An ocean rower himself, Justin had previously built *Darien*, the boat that Damo rowed solo from the Canary Islands in 2017.

The *Cushlamachree* was designed to self-right if capsized. It was a foam sandwich construction – fibreglass, foam, fibreglass – with compartments, so that one end of it could have a big hole in it and take in water, but it would still be fine. Its small compact shape meant it would be easier to manoeuvre in bad conditions. There was a supply cabin, and our own snug cabin would also store the batteries, electronics and our watermaker, so we could access everything even if we had to stay under cover. The initial design was for one rower at a time, but Justin later adapted it to allow the two of us to row side by side if we needed to double up the power.

New Year 2021 was a difficult time for everyone because of the pandemic. I think everyone's mental health was at a low. It had come and gone and I hadn't felt like setting any goals or targets. However, I quickly decided to revert back to what I knew made me tick. I set myself a challenge, a 216km virtual row from Athenry to the NRH. I got a rowing machine from Gabe Cronnelly and started tearing into it. Gabe, a local politician and an amputee, was another graduate of the NRH. There's a charity, CrewBlu, that teaches people with disabilities to row and paddle, and Gabe got me involved, taking me along the canals in Galway city. It was the first time I had been in a canoe or kayak.

I was constantly looking out for things to keep me motivated. A little three-year-old girl named Katie Walsh had had her lower leg amputated after a lawnmower accident, and people were doing everything to fundraise for this girleen, so I decided to do something as well. In July 2021 I set out to row seven marathons in seven days, and I did it. Every row was under 3 hours 10 minutes and all but one were under three hours. That achievement felt good, considering where I had started from – just enough stamina for five minutes in the District Gym.

After getting up Diamond Hill I had also wanted to climb more mountains, so I set my sights on Croagh Patrick, where I had taken many bus tours over the years. I tackled it on my own that same month and it was very slow going. It was cloudy when I got to the top, so I didn't get that incredible view of Clew Bay that first time, and I came down mostly on my arse, but it was a wonderful feeling to make it up, and down. Anything that challenged me was helping me improve.

I felt I was absolutely flying it.

Damo and his partner Rozelle had a baby girl, Elodie, in early April 2021. They had moved back to Australia to be with Rozelle's family for support, and getting in and out of Australia was particularly difficult during COVID. Within days of the birth he had left for an attempt on Mount Everest. The plan had been that they would return to Ireland for six months before the row. They did come back but had to return to Brisbane again when they couldn't find a house to rent or get Rozelle insured to drive. He said he would be back for a six-week training window, but it felt like the rug had been pulled from under me, that I was on my own.

Damo had a training programme that suited him perfectly and he wanted me to do it too. But his programme was unsuitable for me. Because of issues with blood flow, heavy leg sessions could take me a couple of weeks to recover from. However, when I was doing my own thing, I was doing really well, making progress slowly but very surely.

By the end of 2021 I was out of the bus business. I was fully committed to Project Empower, but the funds we needed weren't coming in. The pandemic was playing even further havoc with our plans. Sponsors had pulled out, and there was no sign of new ones. We couldn't even afford to pay for half the boat, so I got my dad to lend some money he had received from selling the business to keep the project on track until we got the sponsors we needed, when it was repaid. However, I still felt I was not a partner in any way. In my head it seemed to me that it was Damo and MacDara who called every shot, that I couldn't question anything.

Damo returned to Ireland for our six-week training block in December 2021. He arranged to meet me in a coffee shop in Oranmore, but brought photographer Emilija along, and started recording for his podcast. I didn't show it, but in that moment I was taken aback; I almost felt ambushed in a way. He started asking me if I was pushing myself hard enough. I played along, saying I supposed I could push myself harder, and he started going on about how he was here to help me now. My back was up. Whatever his good intentions I felt that he always wanted to appear as the one helping me, and in my mind I was thinking, 'You fucked off and left me. I've been training my way and doing great.'

We had set up a gym in my garage because he had a lot of gym equipment. He might tell me he would be out at 12 o'clock but wouldn't arrive until four, and he'd never let me know. Everything was on his terms. And while his programme was incredibly impressive for an able-bodied person, it just wasn't suitable for my legs. I was going nowhere. He was doing weekly progress checks and sometimes I was even going backwards because my legs were not recovering. He wanted me to do heavy leg day after heavy leg day, and I just couldn't do that because of issues with my blood circulation and lack of sensation – even a microtear in a muscle takes much longer to heal for me. I was trying to say this to him but any time I tried his response was, 'Have you ever rowed an ocean before? No? I have.' It felt like I was constantly being put in my place, so it got to the stage where I didn't feel I could ask anything. He had done this before, and I didn't want to let myself down. I was also excited at the thought that I was going to row across the Atlantic Ocean, and it was Damo who was giving me this amazing opportunity.

In January 2022, when the boat was finished, Justin brought it over. There was an official unveiling of the boat with Niall Breslin, 'Bressie', a former rugby compatriot of Damo's, as MC. Then we launched from Renville into Galway Bay. That was a day we were meant to be out learning, but it was cut short. To fundraise, an opportunity to row with us on the launch had been sold. We rowed out with the woman who had paid for the privilege, but when we turned to come back in, the winds were against us. It took us about 15 minutes to get out, and two hours to get back in. It was an eye-opener to me. I was rowing hard and digging in but I was only moving 200 metres or so.

Justin stayed for a few days. We realised very quickly that because we were two wide men our hips were rubbing up against part of the boat when we sat side by side, if we needed to double up rowing. Justin would have to bring the boat back to England to make modifications. We did only one overnighter in Galway Bay, out to Rossaveal, before the boat went back.

Damo stayed for six weeks and then returned to Australia. The plan had been to spend four or five nights out over the Irish Continental Shelf, but it never happened. The one night we spent on Galway Bay, the sea was like glass, picture perfect. He had to go back to Rozelle and Elodie; that was important for them as a family, and he had promised not to be away for any longer. However, it meant that we weren't prepared; I wasn't prepared for what lay ahead. The first time I would be out in an ocean would be when we left Manhattan. Everything else was done in the gym, which wasn't the plan. However, I wasn't aware of the implications that lack of preparation might have when we began the row. I trusted Damo's expertise.

The boat had to be shipped from England to New York, and I was soon flat out sorting out stuff. I went back and forth to Devon, which was a 14- or 15-hour trip from Galway via Fishguard. I'd get the boat, bring it back, test it, and then bring it back to England again for modifications. I enjoyed all the toing and froing because it was an important part of the project and I'm good at the logistics stuff. That's my business. Damo, meanwhile, continued working really hard getting sponsorship, coming up with good ideas, and building up followers on social media, which wasn't my forte. The next time we would meet would be in New York.

My family thought I was nuts to take on the row, though Attracta was very supportive. I had put my family through a lot of hardships because of my accident, the financial crash of my business, the end of my relationship, and the suicide attempt. So while I was doing this very positive thing, it still ended up causing my loved ones a lot of grief. They were very worried about what I was doing, but they also had to put plans into action to help me out. I put so much more work on them,

As departure time came closer I could see Bradley was nervous about it. I had brought the boat back to Ireland to get it branded and to load up supplies and equipment. I got him to help me pack the boat in my yard, so he could see it was going to be safe, and what I was going to be eating – we needed to bring 10,000 calories worth of food a day for 60 days. Meanwhile, Aimee, who usually keeps her emotions to herself, became more huggy, more affectionate, as the time got closer to me leaving.

I brought the boat back to England to be shipped. On 28 May 2022 I had done everything I could from Ireland. It was time to get on a plane to New York. I didn't have a return ticket. I would be rowing home!

DON'T EVER UNDERESTIMATE YOUR ABILITY. CAN THE CAN'TS.

As human beings it is our minds that hold us back. The body can be trained to reach its limits, and to find new limits, though they will be different for everyone. I have no time for 'I can't …' before someone even tries. We all underestimate our ability to do things, to push ourselves. No matter what our limitations are, we can achieve more than we ever thought possible.

20

ANXIETY IN NEW YORK

In New York we were given amazing suites at the Fitzpatrick hotel, thanks to Dave McCormack, who was originally from Castlebar. I had been on a Connacht Competitions committee with his father Johnny. Dave sponsored that accommodation, among other things. It was a lot of money.

However, finances were very tight. We only secured our final sponsor a week or two before arriving in New York and it just about covered our costs. I had told Damo I wasn't bringing any family over because it would cost too much money, so I would be on my own. His parents, Joe and Mary, visited for a few days, but Rozelle and Elodie had accompanied him, and because he was with them a lot I was left to my own devices, often waiting for hours for him to appear. I was extremely lonely. I was hours and days on my own. I would have jumped at any opportunity even to have breakfast with someone. I was glad to see any familiar face.

Once again, I felt that everything had to be done Damo's way. I didn't feel my opinion was valued on anything. At first the boat was in New Jersey and we were stationed in Manhattan, and it was a big ordeal to get there and back, and we'd be going over and doing a couple of hours and coming back. I suggested we spend a day there and get everything sorted in one go, but the response was 'No'. It had to be done his way. The way I remember it, he seemed to need to micromanage everything. I even felt humiliated when he was handing me $200 here and there to get stuff for the row. We were about to row across an ocean together and I felt that he wouldn't even trust me with a project credit card.

I came from a place where I had been in charge of a business, and had built teams, so it was hard for me to take a back seat all the time, but I did. If I questioned anything at all the response was: 'Have you rowed an ocean before?' It was constantly made clear that Damo and MacDara were running the show. It was always two against one. In the end I was so worn down I let myself become a total yes-man, which is so not me. I also realise now that I am someone who needs a bit of craic, a bit of fun, no matter how serious my purpose is, even if it is just a bit of silly banter, to relieve tension. And there was no craic at all.

While I had been depressed before, I had never before experienced ongoing anxiety. But over there, I felt completely isolated and the anxiety just grew from all the hanging around. It was crippling. I couldn't sleep. Everything seemed a big ordeal. Waiting around all the time, and not knowing what was happening next, made me feel I had no control. That feeling of anxiety would continue to hold me in its grip for a long time afterwards. Even thinking about that time now makes me feel edgy. I had never felt so disempowered in my life. I really don't think Damo ever realised that I felt I had no control, or the impact that was having on me, or how stressful I was finding hanging around waiting for him. We should have communicated more, but neither of us is good at that. I'm sure he thought he was doing things the right way, while I had just wanted to be on the row so badly, I had just accepted everything when I shouldn't have.

One of my toughest days was when I knew Bradley was making his First Communion. I had bought him the suit before I left. Seeing the photos from home just set me off. I walked up to Central Park, alone and in tears. I was missing this once-off landmark moment in my son's life. I felt guilty and upset, and wanted comfort, but there was none.

In February 2022 I had gone to Paris to watch a rugby match. Afterwards, in a bar, I started chatting to a woman. Fernanda was from Brazil and had lived in Ireland when she was younger. She knew Ireland and Irish people and we had stayed chatting. When she asked me what I did, I told her I was going to try and row an ocean, and about my accident and injury. She told me later that this had really spiked her interest in me as a person, that she was attracted to the mindset of a person who would be taking on that kind of challenge. She was extremely fit herself. She had swum for Brazil's youth team, and was very involved in CrossFit. We stayed in contact, and two weeks later she visited Ireland for a couple of nights. She had always wanted to see the Cliffs of Moher, so I brought her there. And then I went to see her in Paris. She was just after a break-up and was also very lonely. They had moved to France just before COVID hit, and she ended up alone with her baby for a lot of that time. Her loneliness resonated with me. Things just aligned when we met, and we fell in love. We talked all the time, and I kept her up to date about the project and everything that was going on. When Fernanda realised how low I was feeling in New York, she flew over to be with me for a few days, and it was such a relief to have someone with me.

I was also so happy to see the documentary team – Tomek, Emilija and Boyd Challenger – when they arrived. It was a breath of fresh air to have other people around, and it was fun and exciting to be going around New York with two massive oars and a film crew! There are great photos of us in Times Square, but when I look at them they prompt an unwelcome memory, which illustrates how many repercussions of my spinal injury still dog me. As we were posing for the pictures I realised I needed the bathroom, but they wanted another shot, and another … We were in an iconic location, this was an important moment, so instead of saying I had to go, I held on, which I should never do. Eventually I told them, 'I have to go' and got to a Starbucks on a corner as quickly as I could. But they had just cordoned off the bathrooms. As I tried to figure out where to go next my bowels started to release and I was wearing beige shorts. I got myself to a hotel lobby and luckily a woman saw my predicament and pointed me towards the toilets. I rang Damo and asked him to bring my bag of spare clothes and wipes that I always carried with me. I left that hotel about 45 minutes later with my head hanging in shame. It was a rude reminder of how my body could let me down. I could never fully relax.

I had also started shutting myself away at that stage, when there wasn't something to be done, when I felt I didn't have a purpose. I now know that if I stop socialising and communicating with people, depression is on its way. I know how to react to it now, but then I didn't. I just shut myself off. Even when someone from the crew said they were going to the shop, I wouldn't go with them. I'd wait and go ten minutes later so I could avoid making conversation.

But even in the midst of all that mental turmoil there were so many great moments. We had some training sessions rowing on the Hudson, which is a really busy river. We had negotiated our way around and between ferries, yachts and commercial vessels and even around the Statue of Liberty, which was just a surreal experience.

Damo had always told me that things were going to be manic leading up to the departure, but I had no idea of just how manic it would get, and how much anxiety and stress that brought on us. In addition to running around in the heat, getting the last bits of equipment, there were lots of events and PR that had to happen. We were even filmed for a spot on prime time news, and gave a talk at the famous New York Athletics Club. After that talk, someone offered us a berth at Chelsea Piers, and that made logistics a bit easier. Our little green *Cushlamachree* was bobbing alongside some spectacular yachts, where people held parties without even casting off. Everyone seemed fascinated by us and what we were planning, but I didn't have enough time to soak it all in.

Both our tempers became frayed – Damo was obviously frustrated with me too – and a row finally erupted at the pier over packing the boat and the counterbalance. We hugged it out afterwards, but we just had to get on with it. Perhaps if we had time, we should have sat down and talked more before we set off, but I think if we had started we wouldn't have been able to stop, and that might have caused more problems than it solved.

Chris Martin from New Ocean Wave was our weather router and on-the-ground support, an amazing guy, and really well respected in the ocean rowing world. He would be on call for us for any issues throughout the row. He explained how important it was for us to get into the Gulf Stream as early as possible. This would bring us into safer, deeper water, allow us to go more quickly, and reduce the risk of coming into contact with hurricanes blowing up the coast.

Bad weather postponed our initial departure date of 8 June, and again on 10 June. Now we were to row out with the tide on the morning of 13 June, but we were delayed again when we realised the night before that our satellite phone didn't work – and that would be essential for our safety, for communicating with the world. A man we had met at the New York Athletic Club drove me around for hours to try to find a new one, but there wasn't one to be found in New York. Then a guy Damo had met on Everest, Akash Negi, also got involved with the search. A new one was finally located in Pennsylvania – a five-hour drive away. Akash drove us down to pick it up, and it worked! I napped in the car for about half an hour – my nerve pain levels had shot up, which always happens when I am under pressure – but when we finally headed for Chelsea Piers to row out with the night tide, we had barely slept for 36 hours.

WATCH FOR YOUR WARNING SIGNS.

Learn the warning signs, the signals, of when you are feeling low, or struggling mentally. Don't bottle up feelings or concerns. I still struggle to communicate, to talk things out when I have an issue but I'm constantly trying to improve.

21

ALL AT SEA

We left from Pier 59 in Chelsea Piers, pushing off in the dark just after 10 p.m. on 13 June, ahead of the turning tide. I was so tired that I can barely remember our departure, or who was there, but as we set off there was music playing, and Irish flags, and people cheering us off. As we rowed out, a tiny silhouette against the lights of the massive Manhattan skyline behind us, I just drank in the moment. I didn't think beyond the next few hours. I just enjoyed that we were finally on our way.

We rowed down the Hudson along the west side of Manhattan Island, passing Battery Park, Lady Liberty, Governors' Island. We could hear regular shouts of encouragement from land, and a small crowd had gathered at the bottom of Manhattan Island, playing Irish music, running along the embankment and calling out good luck wishes. Then we were under the Verrazzano-Narrows Bridge and into the North Atlantic.

A couple of hours out the rowing got harder, and our speed dropped, from about six knots down to one. We were also 12 hours behind our weather window. The forecast wasn't great. Chris had told us there was some bad weather up ahead, and we had hoped to get ahead of it. We knew the hardest part of the row would be from New York to the Gulf Stream, fighting the Labrador Current coming down from Newfoundland, onshore winds and tides. Our route would also take us to the bottom of the Grand Banks – I knew about those from the film *The Perfect Storm*. This first section was the part where most people failed.

I was still racked with anxiety, but it was all from the build-up to our departure. I felt no fear whatsoever heading off to navigate an ocean in that small vessel. There would not be one day, one second, when I felt unsafe on that boat. It just wasn't a fear that ever entered my head. I had seen Justin build *Cushlamachree*. I had seen his craftsmanship. I knew she could withstand anything, that if we capsized she would roll and self-right again. We might get tossed about a bit, but it couldn't be far. I had visualised that, and it didn't scare me at all.

I was also filled with anxiety about the unknown. I have since heard Damo talk about how much time he had spent in Galway Bay before his first row. I hadn't even a couple of days under my belt. And he had experience of a solo row, not one with a companion. I knew setting off that the first few weeks were going to be a challenge, because we would be getting used to our routines; we would be in very uncomfortable surroundings; and though we had spent a lot of time together as mates, it had never been at such close quarters. Both of us, particularly me, had a lot to learn.

For the first ten or eleven hours we rowed one hour on, one hour off. We knew we'd be giving it the most output per shift if we kept it to one hour. Then we increased the shifts to one and a half hours, and then to two, to try to catch up on some sleep.

Damo had warned me about the probability of being constantly wet and cold, so I was expecting that, but I wasn't expecting the heat. The sun beat down relentlessly from morning to night; it was about 30 degrees. In the cabin it was even more extreme. We had to keep it airtight, with the hatches closed, when the sea was rough, and the sun turned the fibreglass compartment into a sauna. It was like being inside a car with all the windows closed during an Irish heatwave. During breaks from rowing, we would go inside the cabin, take off our clothes because we had to, and still be in a lather of sweat. It wasn't a break. The anxiety became crippling. I'd be in there, barely able to breathe, hoping it would soon be time to get back outside to row, to any kind of breeze.

Within 24 hours we were a good bit out into the Northern Atlantic Ocean – we had rowed about 47 nautical miles – but then a bad weather front came in and we hit our first big wind. We were forced to put down the power anchor and go into the cabin together. You had to do that if the wind was anything above 25 knots. There's absolutely no point in rowing in winds like that because you make no gains, so you go into the cabin to reserve energy. That was when I realised how difficult things could get. It was also when I discovered I had severe claustrophobia. The cabin was two metres long, and it was 0.7, 0.8 metres high at the highest point. It was shaped like a cone, so you went in at the widest part, and the other end was the tip.

I am the smaller man, at six foot one, so I drew the short straw. My head was down at the top of the cone. I always sleep on my side but that wasn't possible there because I would have been tossed back and forth. So when I was on my back, the ceiling of the boat was less than a foot away from me. The condensation was dripping down on my face, and my own hot breath was bouncing back down. If I turned my head to the left the side of the boat was no more than a foot away from me. If I turned to the right I had Damo's feet up against my face. The cabin was roasting. There was no air going through at all, and it was so difficult for either of us to manoeuvre.

I think we spent eight or nine hours in the cabin that first time. He never offered to change places and give me a break, and I never asked. I should have. It was so overwhelming that three times, despite that wind, I had to break out of the cabin, open up the hatch, get fresh air, and eventually coax myself back inside. That was dangerous. There was a moment each time when you had to unclip your lanyard to open the latch, and there was a huge risk of going overboard. If I had been separated from that boat I would have been dead, but I had to get out. I was really struggling. I was just a mess of anxiety. The only thing that kept me going was telling myself, 'It's not going to last. It's not going to last,' and focusing on my breathing as much as I could.

Once we got rowing again I immediately picked up. I have a good mentality whereby I can get on with the next thing, push what happened behind me, and move on. That doesn't mean I don't think about it; I just move on to the next thing and concentrate on that. And that's what I did.

We had to go into the cabin together twice more because of the weather, before we made a decision that we would do everything to avoid doing it again. We chose to keep rowing, even when we were making virtually no progress, rather than dropping the power anchor and reserving energy in the cabin. It was horrendously tough, but we made a decision that since we were big powerful men, much bigger than most ocean rowers, we could get a little bit more power into our strokes and keep us moving. There was no way we were going back into that cabin together again; it was just too tight. So we rowed through weather and waves that nobody else would have rowed through, making no gains, rather than go back in that cabin together.

During the day, we would do shorter shifts, sometimes an hour on and an hour off, so we wouldn't be out in the sun for too long, burning up way too much energy. Then in the evening, maybe seven or eight o'clock, we'd start stretching out the shifts into the longer night ones. During those shorter shifts, by the time you had everything done and yourself dried down and maybe a bite to eat and some water taken it was almost time to come back out. The cabin never felt like a sanctuary for me. The minute I went inside I was drenched in sweat, and because there were two air hatches, even when you lay down, the sun would be glaring in your face.

I was having anxiety attacks about going into the cabin, and anxiety attacks about having to come back out again, usually prompted by the five-minute call to start getting ready to take over on the oars again. I already knew that being on a boat rocking back and forth, and having severely reduced proprioception, was going to be an issue for me. But it was worse than I imagined, and it made me very anxious standing up, and about possibly falling overboard. At times our tiny boat was among 20-foot waves, with side-on winds, and this made moving from the cabin to our rowing seat a tremendous effort, even for Damo, who had none of my issues. My chest was just full of anxiety all the time. But every time I just got through it, and once I was back on the rowing seat, back on the oars, there was a sense of relief. There was a breeze on my face. We were making progress. I had something to do. I put on my headphones, my music and off I went.

The rowing was the easy part. I was out in the fresh air and had something to do. But it was extremely tough. Every wave, which means one every second, can completely manipulate your boat, and it could take ages to get back on course. A lot of the time we were fighting just to keep the boat going in the right direction. And while we were really pushing hard that first week, trying to get the nautical miles underneath our belts, I was also on a massive learning curve. Learning to manoeuvre around the boat, to use and empty our toilet (a bucket with a toilet seat on top), to make and eat food, to ensure I was constantly hydrated.

My balance was so much worse with the motion of the waves. I repeatedly banged my head off the side of the boat. I would burn my hands trying to pour boiling water into the sachets of food. There was nothing easy about living on a boat in the middle of the ocean. If we had spent the five days over the Irish Continental Shelf that we had planned, that would have given me so much insight into what life would be like – a rehearsal for the two of us of living in close quarters together – and so much understanding of what was in front of me. Not only the rowing, but the rowing on top of the lack of sleep, the motion of the boat, the lack of food. I wasn't too bothered by sea sickness, but it did affect our appetites and made all the food taste horrible – like cardboard. Not wanting to eat also contributed to fatigue, and we had been exhausted even before leaving New York.

I hadn't understood another difficulty I would encounter. The boat was far too small to allow us to walk around upright. It's so hard to describe to anyone who has normal function in their lower body, but I have zero strength when I am in an unusual, non-upright position.

Being on my hunkers, and getting up and down, is the most difficult position for me. When I am down on my hunkers I am extremely weak. All my efforts since my accident had been about keeping myself upright. I hadn't myself trained for bending down, or hunkering down – which was the position I needed to be in constantly as I negotiated carefully around the boat.

Even today, getting up and down off my knees or the ground is the hardest movement for me to complete, for my brain and my body to process. Now I had to do this constantly as the boat rocked. I was on my hands and knees, trying to find footholds in very confined spaces. It was almost like crawling around a tunnel. And then, because I would be in such an awkward position, I would have no power in the other foot to drive myself off and go forward another step. My body was continuously having to learn to move from new angles Every moment required a huge exertion, and constant concentration. And it meant digging deep into my stores of stamina. It was exhausting.

Even getting in and out of the cabin was an ordeal, requiring me to take up unnatural positions. Inside there was a well for our feet, and getting out I had to lean out first, and then power myself up. In the gym I could nail repeated squats and deadlifts but these are exercises that are controlled and in a specific direction – you never do a squat with your leg contorted. I could have the strongest thighs and calves and glutes in the world, but once I was in an awkward position none of them talked to each other. Even if I had trained every part of my body on land, these positions would never have arisen. They were unique to the small confines of this little vessel in the middle of the ocean.

I didn't make an issue about it, because I was still able to get around, but I had to think about every movement. The only place where I didn't need to think was on those oars; my body had been trained to row. But even then I had to concentrate on what direction the next wave was coming from. No two strokes are the exact same. For one pull of the oars the wave might be to your left, and that meant your left oar would be up in the air, and your right oar would be deep in the water. But the next stroke might require the opposite. Even people who row on rivers will find that difficult to understand. Ocean rowing throws up a whole range of variables aside from using your power to pull on the oars. I hadn't realised the full enormity of that. When I had been out on Galway Bay the surface had been like glass. The waves on our currach row from Inisheer to Galway had given me a hint of what we might face, but they were miniscule to what we were encountering in this part of the Atlantic. But that's not me moaning. Despite, or maybe because of, the exertion, I actually loved the rowing. I enjoyed computing where to put my stroke and where to use my strength.

It became my sanctuary. As someone with virtually no feeling below the belly button, rowing suited me so well. My feet were anchored in. They were in front of me and I could see them, identify with them. I had five points of contact to help my brain compute where my body was. I was sitting on my backside. My two hands were gripping the oars. My two feet were pushed down onto the floor of the boat, and that pressure through my feet actually eased the nerve pain. I was quite content.

I'm not big into music, but Fernanda had put a long playlist together for me – deep house, Brazilian, dance – a lot of which was up-tempo and gave me great energy when I was rowing. I also had my own music, including Johnny Cash, Christy Moore, the Saw Doctors; and I was trying to learn Portuguese. The hours I spent on the seat were my best hours. I felt useful. I felt challenged. My mind was occupied.

I was in my element a lot of the time while I was rowing, but it was tough and relentless. However, I had geared myself up for that. What I hadn't factored in was another element. My body is in excruciating nerve pain every second of the day, and that leads to fatigue. And that was something I had never thought of, that on top of being exhausted from the physical exertion, I would be exhausted from that constant effort of my body fighting pain. Damo didn't understand that either, and I didn't try to make him understand. I should have been more vocal and tried to communicate that to him. However, I thought I was really pulling out the stops in terms of the amount of mileage I was getting in. Maybe on his side, he thought I was lacking, but I knew I was giving it my all, and I also knew that Damo, by his nature, would be giving it his all.

Damo was doing a podcast every day, so his focus was on that and the challenge, and not on the relationship between himself and myself. At times I found that difficult, though I never said or did anything about it. It was a lonely enough experience, because one rowed while the other was in the cabin, and when we were together we were too tired to talk. Our chat was mainly about how we had slept, our speeds, the chores and tasks that needed doing. When one of us asked, 'How are you getting on?' it wasn't an invitation to start a deep and meaningful conversation.

However, from day eight I felt I was improving. I was getting used to it all, the rowing, living in a confined space, never really standing up. I was getting more comfortable, beginning to settle into a routine, to get into the swing of things. We had rowed south-east out of New York, as if we were heading towards the Canary Islands, to get into the Gulf Stream. There's never a guarantee that you are going to get into the Gulf Stream, so to row away from Ireland to get into it was a big risk. Thankfully, the risk paid off.

PERSEVERANCE IS EVERYTHING.

Getting knocked down again and again shouldn't stop you from getting back up. It's tough but it's possible. Keep remembering in those bad moments that this too will pass.

22

THE GULF STREAM

Once we got into the Gulf Stream we could feel the power of it straight away. We were now rowing at four or five knots per hour, barely tapping the water. Prior to that, when we were just on the edges of it, we had only been managing a maximum of two knots per hour, sometimes only half a knot per hour. We were absolutely flying it now, and I think we felt that some of the hard work was done and the next 15 days might be easier for us.

But it was time to push myself again. One of the things I had been dreading was having to get into the ocean. I knew we would need to do it to clean ourselves and, even more important, to clean the barnacles off the boat because they would slow us down. I had thought a lot about it. When my legs are in water I do not know where they are, and they feel weightless. I really struggle to swim – I couldn't even swim well before the accident – because I don't know whether my feet are behind me or being dragged. Therefore it's no surprise that the idea of being separated from contact with the boat was giving me the heebie jeebies.

But day nine or ten was lovely. The weather was good, the mood was good, we were making progress, and Damo, who doesn't swim well either, got ready to take the plunge. He asked if I was going to go in, but I really wasn't comfortable. We could see from the pedometer that it was 4,900 metres deep at that point and to drop into the ocean knowing it is that deep is hard to get your head around.

As Damo hopped in a school of dolphins passed by, and that was so cool. He spent about ten minutes cleaning off the barnacles, then told me, 'Come on, give it a go.' So I decided, 'Fuck it, I will', and within a few minutes I was in the water. The dolphins had kept going, but when I got in, at the back of my mind was the thought that they might circle back, and that was exciting. However I still kept a grip on the side of the boat, even though I was attached to it by a lanyard.

I quickly realised how easy it was to float, because of the salt content of the water, and the buoyancy aid, so I just lay back and relaxed. It was a rare moment to get the opportunity of feeling complete muscle relaxation; that my body was light and weightless. I even submerged and got a few barnacles off, though there was still an element of fear; fear of what might be below me. Getting into the ocean was a bigger fear than the rest of the challenge, because there's always an unknown – something could come up and bite you!

I was only in the water for 10 or 15 minutes, but it was just a wonderful sense of calm. I felt a huge sense of relief, and release, and was delighted I had got in. It was one of the few moments on the row when I thought, 'This is lovely.' But then there was the realisation that I had to get back into the boat, which is difficult, especially when you don't have feelings in your lower body; for instance, when I throw my leg up I don't know if it is high enough. It was Damo who pulled me in. But what an experience; scary and surreal but also exciting and exhilarating.

Rowing at night there was always the added bonus of watching the moon and the sky with its dazzling show of stars. Now there was the added distraction of flying fish. I had always thought they were a myth, but they were very real. They would land with a wallop in our lap, or slap us in the face before floundering around the boat. We didn't want them to die, so we would have to get up from our rowing position, catch them and throw them back over the side. They were slippery suckers, so that took a while, but they were beautiful, a spectacular iridescent blue-green colour. It was very cool, but by the time I'd managed to get the fish out of the boat, and get back in the rowing position on the seat with my feet in the stirrups, four or five minutes might have passed, and it would take a while to get back on course again. And that could happen two or three times in a two-hour shift.

By day 11 we were still on target to break the record. However, as our ocean life got easier, I started failing. It was still very warm and I had noticed that I was getting very tired very quickly. There had been talk about getting blisters on my hands and about body pains, but I wasn't sore, just tired. My hamstrings were in great shape, so were my calves, my quads, my shoulders, my back, my arms. I wasn't sore anywhere. The rowing at that stage was still blissful, but I just couldn't do it for long any more, because I didn't have the energy. I didn't mention anything to Damo. I did my shift, but my performance was way down. I was beginning to have to take breaks, doing maybe 10 or 15 strokes, taking the oars out of the water and taking a 10-second break before I could start again.

My vision was also beginning to be affected. That night the sky was cloudy so we couldn't navigate by looking at the stars. We had an Astra compass to keep us on track, and we would shine a torch on it to check our direction, but now I noticed that I was struggling to see it. I'd have to stop, my knees in the rowing position, look and then come back. In the cabin I tried to sleep but only managed half an hour. I remember thinking, had I not hydrated enough, or eaten enough? Even though I had been drinking loads of water, on my next break I drank more, to see if it was dehydration; when we had gone out onto Galway Bay I had got a severe headache from dehydration. We hadn't been eating well, so on the next break I forced food into myself. But nothing worked. The last straw was on my next shift. I ate a big chocolate bar, some nuts, and a big bag of Haribo jellies just to give myself an energy boost, but there was nothing. I was still flat.

As we went into the second night of me feeling unwell, I still hadn't said anything to Damo, but I'm sure he noticed I was flagging. I was sure I would get my energy back. I was just flat out on each break, even sleeping for longer stretches. When we swapped places I would see he had done five knots or more in his two hours. But by the time I had got set up and taken one stroke I was drained. I was falling over the oars. There was no life left in me. Damo would come out and I'd only have 500 metres done, in the Gulf Stream – which would take you 500 metres without even rowing. This went on all night,

My vision became worse. Now I couldn't even manage to see the compass from the seat. I'd have to stop, take my feet out of the straps, get up, look at the compass, get back into the seat, put my feet back into the straps, and pick up the oars. But by the time I had all that done I would be wrecked, and the boat could have been going in any direction because the wind or a wave might have turned us around. Even to keep the boat going in the right direction was becoming impossible. At one stage I knew I was going in the wrong direction because the pedometer was going backwards – I was actually losing ground. I was rowing the wrong way. It just got worse and worse and worse, I was struggling to breathe, having to take two breaths for one pull of the oars. I would do five or six strokes and be exhausted. I was feeling weak and light-headed.

On my last shift I began falling asleep on the oars. I'd just be tapping the water because it was so calm but within a few strokes I'd doze off. I would jolt awake when the oars in the water started pulling at me. I started to lie back on the seat, or on the deck, and would lose track of time. There was absolutely no place to lie that was comfortable, nowhere to lie without having something stick into you, but I didn't care. I couldn't stay sitting up on that seat.

My breathing became worse as the night went on. The left side of my chest began tightening up every time I inhaled. As I lay on the deck feeling sorry for myself, I realised that the last time I had felt like this, with laboured breathing, with this fatigue, was when I had had two massive clots in my lungs at the Mater Hospital. I was having the exact same feeling, no energy, needing really deep long breaths to get anything in, and I thought, 'Oh shit. This cannot be happening to me again.'

I had been told that once you'd had clots you were susceptible to them again. Because of the reduced sensation in my legs my circulation is also reduced, and I had more or less been sitting down in one position most of the time, while I was rowing, and then hunkered down while I was moving around the boat. I was never standing up.

It was getting bright when I decided I needed to check my blood oxygen levels. I knew we had a device, because I had bought it for the medical kit, but finding it was going to be an ordeal. I crawled over to the supply cabin, opened up the locker. It took me ages to find the kit and then I struggled to pull it out from under other supplies, but I finally got it on my finger. My reading was 86. That wasn't good. I knew it needed to be 96 or above.

So I woke Damo immediately and told him, 'I'm in trouble and I'm really worried.' I gave him the machine to get a reading and his was 98 straight away, so I knew the machine was working. I put it back on my finger and it read 88. I thought I was improving, but it didn't climb from there.

I wasn't thinking straight, but I did start worrying about my kids. I had left them to take on the challenge, but I wasn't going to put my life at risk and leave them for good. I told Damo about my history, and he said we had to ring Chris Martin, our on-the-ground support. It was 1 p.m. Irish time on Sunday 26 June when we called Chris on the sat phone and I told Chris my symptoms. He could hear how I was breathing. He said he needed to ring a maritime doctor for me. A short while later we got a call from a doctor and I told him my symptoms and my history, about the clots, and that I was just off blood thinners for about six months. He said, 'What do you want to do?' And I said, 'I can't make a decision like this.' It wasn't a decision I was in any state to make. I told the doctor that I wanted him to make the decision, to tell me what he advised. I really thought he was going to tell me to rest for maybe 10 or 12 hours, do a read of my blood oxygen levels and come back to him – which would have put our record chances in jeopardy – but it can't have been more than 30 seconds later that he was telling me, 'You're gone. You're done.'

I was finished. My heart just sank. Emotions swept over me. I began sobbing and couldn't stop. I found it very hard to digest.

Chris Martin came back on and told us, 'Leave it with me. I'm going to have to contact the Coast Guard and see what ships are around, and it might be an hour or two before I'm back to you.'

Damo and I just sat there and had a good cry together. No matter how irked I had been by him, and him by me, we had been through so much together. It was just devastating. Two years of our lives, two years of preparation gone – and we had been very much on target to beat that world record.

But then I just accepted it. And it was nearly a relief, because I was now finding it even hard to talk. I was feeling worse.

FACE YOUR FEARS.

Getting into the ocean in the Gulf Stream meant facing a fear, but choosing to get into that water was exhilarating, and gave me one of the highlights of my days at sea. It's not surprising that the harder it is for us to attempt something, the greater the feeling of accomplishment it brings.

23

THE RESCUE

As we sat together on the deck of *Cushlamachree* on 26 June 2022, Chris Martin came back on the radio. 'We're going to organise an evacuation for you. Give me an hour or two.' Then he came back to say the US Coast Guard (USCG) were going to come out and get me. They were putting a ship in place where a helicopter could land, refuel, come to me, winch me up, and bring me back.

However, all that was going to be a huge operation, and would take up to 12 hours to organise. So we were to sit tight. We needed to stay in the same position, or we would be out of the Coast Guard's range. We were about 1,000km out, about 540 nautical miles.

I was feeling terrible. I knew I couldn't continue but was apologising to Damo for leaving him facing months of solo rowing. We had talked about what we would do in this scenario before we left New York, and had decided that if he fell ill or needed to stop, I wasn't going to continue, but if something happened to me he would carry on. He had rowed an ocean before and was happier with solitude than me. I hadn't any ocean experience, and I wouldn't have been able to manage that isolation.

We settled down for a long wait. All kinds of worst-case scenarios were flashing through my mind, but I tried not to think about what might be going on in my body, or dwell on the dread of going back into a hospital, or, even worse, the implications for my children if anything happened to me. Then suddenly we heard the CB radio crackle.

'*Hafnia Shenzhen* ... come in, *Cushlamachree*. We are six point five K away from you, do you need rescue?"

'Yes, please. Medical emergency.'

They had heard the Mayday alert from the USCG, had responded to the request for assistance, and were diverting from their course towards us. Their confusion was obvious as they tried to grasp our situation. 'You're a six point two-metre boat? And two people?'

It wasn't long before we saw this massive tanker on the horizon. I discovered later that the *Hafnia Shenzhen* was just under 230 metres long, almost 40 metres wide, and had a gross tonnage of over 43,600. It was steaming towards us. Thankfully the weather conditions were good. There were only light winds and small swells of about a metre. But when the tanker came within 500 metres of us it got rough, to say the least. They anchored down, because if they came to us they would have rolled us over. They placed themselves in position and Damo was actually able to row us right up alongside. Seeing our 6.2-metre boat beside this massive tanker was bloody frightening. It was high stakes. Our boat was made of strengthened carbon fibre, so if anything went wrong it would have been destroyed.

We were so lucky that because it was a new ship, only 18 months old, it had a hydraulic staircase that dropped down the side of the ship right beside where Damo had positioned *Cushlamachree*. Two of the crew came down the staircase to assist me. I wasn't able to get on my feet, so Damo helped me to get over beside it. He held me from underneath, pushing me up onto the staircase by my backside, and the two crew members grabbed me, pulled me up the stairs and helped me onto the deck.

They kept a grip on me all the time, because at this stage I wasn't able to hold myself up. I was very unsteady. I really was feeling out of it, so it was all a bit of a blur, but I'll never forget those first steps being helped along the top deck of the tanker and realising we were about to disappear below. I stopped to tell the crew members who were with me, 'I have to say goodbye.' I looked over the edge, down at Damo below in *Cushlamachree*, and waved 'good luck'. That was the hardest moment for me, waving him off. It was all over. I was done.

The crew got me inside. There were no medical experts on board, but because it was a new tanker they had an emergency medical room, with oxygen and all the equipment needed to read my vital signs. Captain Sanjay Karki and other members of the crew took me in hand. Less than four hours after we made that first call to Chris Martin I was being given oxygen through a mask. They got my blood oxygen level up to about 92 per cent, but once they took the mask off for a while it would drop again. However, I gradually started managing better and within a few hours I had my breath back. I was feeling physically drained but I was no longer struggling to breathe. Someone gave me a satsuma, the first fresh food I'd had after 14 days of dried food. It tasted incredible. They gave me more food, and bit by bit I began to rally. My vision came back. I was able to hold a short conversation.

I discovered that the tanker was actually heading into New York Harbour. Looking back now I realise how lucky I was, how blessed I was, that the *Hafnia Shenzhen* had been so close; that they were so willing to come to my assistance; that the weather had been so good; that they had a hydraulic staircase; that there was a medical room and oxygen on board; that the crew were so kind; and that they were heading for New York.

In the meantime, the USCG was still fully invested in flying me back to a hospital, because of the condition I was in. A few hours later, when I was feeling a little better, a phone call came from a Coast Guard officer.

'Hi, Mr Farrell, I believe you've been taken on board *Hafnia Shenzhen*. We're ready to rock and roll. It's going to be harder to land on a moving ship, but are you ready?'

And my first thought was 'Oh Jesus, I'm feeling better.'

'Is there a big risk to this?' I asked.

'It's going to be dangerous, but you are in grave danger so we can get this done. We're almost set to go, but we need the final call from you.'

Now that I was feeling better, I began thinking about how much it would cost me if the USCG had to come out and get me, and how much it would cost me in an American hospital. Our expedition was an uninsurable risk. I had no insurance, or funds, to cover any of it. So I asked him to let me think about what to do. I rang back half an hour later.

'Call it off. I'm doing good. I have oxygen now and I'm feeling better. I don't want to put you through the hassle.'

'Are you sure? We're ready. The team is here.' Then he asked me again, 'So your final call is we call it off?'

'Yes. Final call.'

But he still rang me back five minutes later just to make sure.

Looking back I occasionally wonder what that might have been like, being taken off by a helicopter. It would certainly have been another once-in-a-lifetime experience, but I reckon getting rescued by the ship was experience enough!

About six hours after I was rescued I recorded a video for social media. Looking back on that I can see that I was really struggling because I was so tired, and my eyes were hurting, but I was so much better. I spent two days on the *Hafnia Shenzhen*. The tanker had been built in 2020 and she was a chemical and oil tanker sailing under the flag of Singapore, but most of the crew were Indian, so the food was Indian, which I love.

I slept and slept, and once I got a bit of energy back, I was able to go around the ship. I was treated like a celebrity, and it turned out to be a brilliant experience. I couldn't possibly have met more hospitable people. They were curious and chatty. They wanted to talk to me, they wanted to take photos, they wanted to know about trying to row across the ocean. They even wanted to peel oranges for me and make sure I was fed and hydrated. I am still in contact with the wonderful captain, Sanjay Karki, and Cliff, the second officer.

It took us two days to get into New Jersey Harbour but I almost never made it back onto US soil.

Paul Cleary was going to meet me outside the port. He was an amazing help to me when I was in New York, prior to rowing out and afterwards. He's a great guy, from Athenry originally. Damo and I played rugby with him in Galwegians and he's an absolute top man. He and his partner Stacy have a pub and a restaurant in Tribeca.

So we got into the dock. And I was so anxious to get off, to meet Paul, and to start the process of getting home, I thought I would just be able to jump off the boat. I had packed up the few things I had, and they told me to sit tight while they did some paperwork. But hours and hours went by and I was still there, just hanging around. I was nearly nine or ten hours in the cabin waiting to get clearance before Captain Sanje said, 'You're all clear to go.'

I had my waterproof bag on my back with all my stuff, and as I began walking I realised how tired, how exhausted I still was. To get off the ship I had to walk from almost one end of the tanker, where the cabin spaces were, to the platform. It was about 200 metres but it took me five minutes, I was so drained. I did the hugs and thanked them all. They had really saved my bacon. However, to get to that platform, which had been raised from the dock, I had to go through another checkpoint – I think it might have been the Port Authority – and the officer in that cabin said he wouldn't let me through as I hadn't proper paperwork. I told him the captain had done the paperwork. I tried to argue with him, but he kept saying 'No'. There was no way he was letting me on that dock.

I started to walk back to the cabins again. I was totally drained and deflated. What I hadn't realised is that while I had flown into the US and my visa had been stamped, technically I hadn't left America because I had departed on a rowing boat from Chelsea Piers, where there were no customs or immigration. Getting back into the US was now an issue.

Luckily, two other officials, a man and a woman, who had been on the ship – I think they were customs – heard my dilemma and my distress. The man walked towards me, took me by the arm and said, 'Hey, come with us. We'll sort this out.' He told the Port Authority guy, 'We have him', took me down onto the docks, told me, 'This never happened', and put me in his car. If he hadn't decided to help I would have had to stay on the *Hafnia Shenzhen* and head back, possibly to India, with them.

The officials remembered that the same thing had happened to a Scottish rower, Duncan Hutchinson. He had had to be rescued by a tanker while crossing the Atlantic a few years earlier, and had also had visa issues. I had actually been talking to Duncan before the row began to get his advice and to pick his brains. But that was one scenario we hadn't discussed! The docks were so big it took about 15 minutes to get to the exit. Paul Cleary was there, and as nice as everyone had been I've never been so glad to see a familiar face.

BE THANKFUL. BE GRATEFUL. BE KIND.

My rescue by the crew of the *Hafnia Shenzhen* confirmed to me how blessed and how lucky we can be even at our most difficult times. They are just some of the many people I have met on this journey that I will be forever thankful for and grateful to. Never underestimate how important and far reaching showing a little kindness can be for others.

24

AFTER THE RESCUE

I started withdrawing, wanting to avoid people, almost straight away. Paul brought me to his apartment in Brooklyn, and took me with him when he was heading into Manhattan, but I was really only fit for bed. Even standing up from a sitting position I was getting dizzy and I hadn't found my land legs again.

I needed to be checked by a doctor, and get a blood test to show I was not clotting, to confirm that I was medically fit and at no risk, so that I would be allowed to fly home. I had no travel health insurance because it's worth nothing for someone like me with a spinal cord injury, as I am excluded from so many different things. Therefore, I did not want to go into a hospital in America and be left with a huge bill. There was no money in the project and I certainly couldn't afford it.

So Paul organised a really good doctor nearby and she gave me the once-over and took some bloods. I told her, 'All I want to know is, am I safe to fly home? When I get home, I'll get everything sorted.' People give out about the health service in Ireland, but I've never had anything but the highest of praise for it. It was coming into the weekend of Independence Day, the Fourth of July. She told me that the bloods needed to go to a lab, and that it could be Tuesday before they came back. My heart sank.

I wasn't feeling great, but I also didn't want to face people. So I booked a hotel for myself. I just wanted to be alone. It was only about 800 metres from Paul's restaurant in Tribeca to the hotel, but it took me around two hours. It was a bad decision to walk. I should have hopped in a taxi but I was afraid to spend money.

I met Paul sporadically after that but otherwise I hid in my hotel room. He and other people like Dave McCormack had helped me out so much in New York, but I was exhausted and I couldn't hold a conversation. These were also the people I had been telling I was going to row across the ocean in world record time. I just couldn't face them. I might go downstairs to get a pizza but then it would be straight back up to the room with the curtains closed. I rebooked a different hotel each night to get the cheapest deals.

In the meantime, Paul's brother Sean in Ireland was on to the Irish Consulate, and Andrew Byrne got in touch, and remained in contact, trying to help sort out any paperwork and to ensure I was okay healthwise. Ciarán Cannon – I think he was a councillor in Galway at the time – also got on to me to make sure I was okay.

I had one lucky break. On the Thursday the doctor called to say the test had come back and I was clear to go. I could fly home. When I looked at flights, tickets to Ireland were colossal money, €2,000–2,500, but I found a flight from Stewart International Airport – about two hours outside New York City – via Reykjavik for half the price. From Reykjavik there was the option to fly to Dublin, Paris or London. I really wanted to see my kids, but I knew they were away with Mandy. If I had flown home they wouldn't have been there. I realised I still didn't want to face anyone. So I flew to Paris, where Fernanda was.

I told everyone in Ireland I had to stay in New York. And I told everyone in New York that I was flying home! That's where my head was at. I was also very worried about my health, and about money. In New York I had probably spent four or five grand over those few days, between flights and accommodation, and nobody from Project Empower had checked to see if I needed financial help. And I never asked for anything. I was too proud.

After two nights I flew to Dublin. I don't even remember who picked me up from the airport, but I do recall the sense of failure that engulfed me. I hid. I kept occupied trying to sort out some work on my grandmother's house, but I didn't want to see anyone. I was at least two weeks home before I even got checked out medically by my GP. The heavy breathing was gone, and I knew I wasn't clotting because of the tests in New York, so I didn't feel there was any urgency.

One thing that kept me going was the supportive messages I received on social media, but it was also two weeks later before I even felt up to posting an Instagram video thanking people – my rescuers, Paul Cleary, our sponsors, Chris Martin. When I did go into town people were trying to console me, to tell me that I had done my best, that my health was my wealth. But though they were trying to be nice, it was just reconfirming to me that I had failed.

I knew I would have been no good to Damian on that boat, that I would have been a liability. But even though I was comfortable I had made the right decision, my mood grew lower and darker. I put it down to the fact that I wasn't able to exercise. Since the accident, exercise and pushing myself had helped keep me mentally strong. However, because I had felt so wrecked, I hadn't been able to go to the gym.

Anxiety was also driving me up the wall, and I kept thinking about the past, thinking about the future. And that's not me.

I had become good about concentrating on the present, and making the most of every moment. I found myself going deeper and deeper into that dark place. It was very tough. The day after I got back I was feeling so bad that I even had to leave Bradley's birthday party early. I was overthinking everything.

It was a call with Fernanda that gave me the kickstart to dig myself out. She knew me when I was in a good place, when I was always making the most of the here and now. Listening to me on the phone, she told me I was causing myself anxiety dwelling on things that weren't in my control, and I needed to start getting myself back into the present. The minute she pointed that out to me, I realised she was right. I was causing myself anxiety because I was worried about my health, worried about what I was going to be doing for work, worried about bumping into people and explaining that I had to leave Damo on the boat.

My mindset changed. I got up and went for a walk with my dogs. I tidied the kids' rooms. I just focused on being with them, on doing positive things, on planning a beach trip with them, and for the first time in weeks I slept well that night.

Leaving *Cushlamachree* was 100 per cent the right decision, because I was three weeks home before I had the energy to even do light exercise again. I continued to tell myself that nothing can prepare you for what's coming for you tomorrow, so I needed to stay in the moment. But despite that conviction that things were on the turn for the better, it was only a brief respite.

Rebuilding anything, including yourself – your physical and mental self – is never going to be an easy or speedy task. It takes time and there will always be setbacks. Recovery is a long process, rarely straightforward, or always positive, and sometimes overwhelming. There will be crashes and breakages, times when the positivity deserts you. However, when those setbacks happen, you will still have made progress, the rebuilding will be further along, even though you mightn't recognise it at the time.

But I didn't understand that. At this stage of my journey, I really didn't accept or acknowledge that what had happened had been out of my control. I was depressed, but I was also very angry. I was angry with myself. I was angry with everything. I continued to fester, to focus my anger on MacDara and Damo, repeatedly playing over scenarios from throughout the project and New York in my head. I was depressed, and when you're depressed you just find things to blame. The anxiety, and pain, and night sweats were making sleep almost impossible, so I had started taking OxyNorm again just to help me fall asleep. I took it for quite a while, and in hindsight I can see that it changed my view of the world, and me as a person at that time, but you don't see that until you stop being a habitual user again.

Even stronger than that anger towards others was a huge sense of failure, of disappointment, of unfinished business, which I just couldn't get over. I still didn't even want to show my face in Athenry. Every time I got a bit of a pickup, I found myself looking back at the 'what ifs'. Did I really need to get off that boat? I was just shredded with doubts. I was also beginning to realise that I also needed to shoulder some responsibility, for not speaking up, for allowing things to rankle. I have been asked how I would have treated a friend who had done the same as me and had to be rescued from that boat. I know I would have treated that person with utmost respect, almost as heroic, for what they had done. But when it's yourself in that situation, that's not the way the mind works.

There were a few things going on. I was doubting myself massively, because I didn't complete the challenge, but I also didn't have a plan, and when I don't have a plan in front of me my brain goes all over the place. And I was exhausted. Between those three things, I was extremely frail mentally. I think it hit so hard because this was the first time since I had grabbed and held on to my new core belief, that every day is a day to improve, that I had pushed my body too far, and I had failed. Up to now I had been up to every challenge. I had used a new mindset and physical conditioning to push myself and win. Now, once again I felt like a failure. It was another failure to add to the list: body, business, marriage, row …

It was a terrible feeling to have left a man out there on that ocean, to have left Damian to do something incredibly difficult on his own. We had told the world we were going to do the row in world record time, and Chris Martin had told us we were on track to get that record. So that knowledge was destroying me as well. We would never get that opportunity again. It's not like running 100-metre sprints; you can try and do that every day. You don't row an ocean every day. Me getting off the boat destroyed all chances, all hope. It was gut-wrenching. We had put in such an effort to get ourselves into that position, and then when we got into the Gulf Stream, and the boat started moving faster with less effort, that's when I had started failing.

I felt I had disappointed people. I felt I had disappointed my family. I felt I had let down a lot of people who had invested their time and money in the project. I had always anticipated being able to come back home after rowing across the Atlantic, possibly setting a world record, and being able to walk around my town and my city with my head held high. Instead, I had only lasted two weeks, and I was walking around with my head lowered.

STOP THE 'WHAT IFS'.

Even though I was haunted by them, one of my pet peeves is people who talk about 'what ifs'. After you make a choice in life you never know what the outcome would have been if you had made a different choice. There is no point in dwelling on what might have been. So much of what happens in our life is out of our control.

25

FACING FAILURE

I tried everything to pull myself out of that dark hole, but nothing was working. My mood was staying low. I was still not right in myself. I was getting short-tempered. I went on holiday to Santorini with Fernanda. We were visiting an old town on the way back to the airport when she kept me waiting. When she finally turned up, and asked me where I had been, I got really annoyed and over-reacted. We argued all the way to the airport, and we almost ended up going our separate ways.

And this was happening with other people too. I could never understand why I would snap. Something would just click in my head and we would end up arguing. I was having these uncontrollable bouts of frustration. I'd snap at people. I was even doing it with the kids. It might only last for 30 seconds, but I'd let out a roar. When you are a big man and you raise your voice, because you are living in your own skin you don't realise that it can be intimidating. It was happening constantly, so I knew I needed help. I'd be trying to get myself out of it, but then I would hide myself away, watching TV, avoiding people.

I finally accepted that I needed to go to the doctor. I went to my doctor, Philip O'Grady, and told him, 'Philip, I'm not good.' He started talking to me, asking me simple questions, like what were my hobbies? Rugby. And when was the last time I had been to a game of rugby? A long time. And when was the last time you were out for a few drinks with your friends? A long time. Are you finding that your chores are building up and building up? Yeah. Are you just leaving things to the very last minute to do? And I was. I'd see things around the yard that would only have taken me five minutes to do, but I'd just walk past them. He told me that what I had was functional depression, and he was going to put me back on antidepressants and see how I got on.

I told him I didn't want any more medication. I was on enough. He explained that it was just another tool to get me back on the road, and I needed to use the tools. I didn't agree, but I was back on to him within a few days, saying, 'I need them. I'll try it.' I was told to be aware that as the antidepressants kicked in my mood would go up and down, and it did.

Fernanda and I would talk every night on the phone, but when we were meeting up we'd end up having stupid arguments. My sense of failure kept feeding into the belief that I wasn't good enough – for her, for anything. It kept nagging and niggling away at me all the time, getting its tentacles into everything I did. Even if I had a silly argument with Attracta I'd think, 'I can't even have a proper relationship with my sister, I'm not good enough even to do that.' If I made a mistake totting up some figures, I lambasted myself for not being good enough. And that didn't go away, even as my brain became accustomed to the medication.

Damo and I had been messaging back and forward after my extraction. However, I knew how difficult it was to text from the boat, and so when he stopped answering I understood. He had bigger things to be worried about than texting me. We were back in touch as he got closer to land. I was really delighted for him. With days to go he was struggling because the weather was going against him, so we were all doing videos for him, to keep him motivated and tell him what a great achievement it was. In October, he arrived into Galway Bay, three months after I had left him, 99 days on his own at sea. *Cushlamachree* had crossed the ocean unscathed. I was so delighted for him, and what he had achieved. I knew it was his immense physical and mental strength that had pulled him through. He really did deserve a hero's welcome. However, I was gutted not to be rowing in with him. The end of the story I had visualised was the two of us rowing into Galway Bay together, side by side.

It was decided he would sit it out at sea that night and come into Galway Docks in the daytime when Rozelle and Elodie could be there. A massive crowd had been organised. However, that night I was with boatbuilder Justin Adkin and Chris Martin, who had stayed with me. About 11.30 or 12.00, Chris's emergency bell started ringing, a distress call from Damo. We all jumped up and hopped in the car. Was he okay? We could see the location, out by Furbo, near where MacDara lived. We sped across town, but by the time we arrived Damo was climbing into an ambulance and the door was closed. The ambulance disappeared.

The *Cushlamachree* had been washed up on the rocks and was firmly stuck. We went down to assess the damage and there was a hole in the side of her, but because she was compartmentalised she could withstand a few holes and stay buoyant.

Luckily Damo was alright, but exhausted, and later that night MacDara told us that the boat would be refloated when the tide rose. The *Cushlamachree* was towed in by the Galway harbour master the next day at noon for a hero's welcome.

I wasn't told anything about the agenda for the day, but luckily people who were close to me knew I wasn't in a good way and they came in around me: Joe Noone, my godson Eoin Caulfield, Alex Dolan, Willie Parker. I was just hanging back. I felt so out of place. When Damo arrived he got a huge ovation, which was brilliant. But while I was delighted for him, a wave of regret and failure flooded over me, that I wasn't on that boat, that I wasn't part of the celebrations. But I had to put on a good face, because he had achieved it, and I hadn't. I was standing back; I could see how exhausted Damo was after his ordeal. Alex told me to go over to him, but I kept saying, 'It's his day, his moment. I don't want to intrude on that.' However, Alex forced me to go over, telling me I would regret it if I didn't. I went over and we hugged and that was lovely. I really was thrilled for him, and happy to see him home and safe.

There were photos taken of the two of us together, and shortly afterwards Damo was brought away, because everybody was on top of him. There was something put on in the Harbour Hotel for him, but I didn't know about it, so we went and had a few pints in O'Connell's on Eyre Square.

There was a reception in the Galmont Hotel that night and I was told about that. I answered a few questions from the stage, but left early to pick up Fernanda from Dublin Airport. I kept away from Galway for the next few days. The whole thing wasn't sitting well with me. It was getting me down. That was the start of me going downhill again, and not being able to put the brakes on. Damo had done what we were meant to do together, and he had done it on his own. And there was this fanfare when he came in, which he deserved; but it made me feel like even more of a failure.

It had taken me a long time to recover from the row. I was in bits. So I couldn't understand how Damo, after 112 days out at sea, could keep going at an incredible pace in the weeks after arriving home. He was functioning like his body hadn't been through an ordeal. Weeks after I had got off the boat – after less than 13 days – I wasn't able to do anything that took a physical toll on me. Months later my blood oxygen levels were still only at 96 or 97 per cent, instead of 98 or 99. I still wasn't able to exercise properly. Damo, however, seemed to be the powerhouse he always had been.

I had a few obligations with sponsors of Project Empower, and Damo was busy with press and other obligations. Then I started seeing stuff on social media, him talking about how a sense of forgiveness had come over him as he came past the Aran Island: 'I forgave Fergus.'

The first time we met properly after he came back was in Fat Tony's coffee shop, to film for the documentary. When the cameras were on he said, 'I'm sorry, Fergus.' I thought I was the one who should be saying sorry. I was the one who had left him on the boat. But he seemed to be apologising for all the things he had said about me on social media and in his podcast. I had never listened to his podcast, and obviously he had a lot of built-up frustration, which was completely understandable. However, if he had something to apologise to me for I felt it should be in person over a pint or coffee, not on social media or on camera. I was annoyed. He should have spoken to me one on one, man to man.

Tomek had come and talked to me on and off camera after I came home, for the documentary, and I had vented a lot of my frustrations to him. I was so angry at the time. I had believed that if you apply yourself everything is possible. That was the message I had been trying to send out to other people who might find themselves in a similar position to mine, but I felt that message had been buried, and that I hadn't delivered on that belief.

A few days later MacDara rang me to say they wanted to close Project Empower. I went in and met them and there was a bit of chit-chat. Then they started talking about doing a show, and that they wanted me involved. They had obviously discussed and agreed it all beforehand, and MacDara said what should happen is that Damien would get 60 per cent of the profits, he would get 25 per cent and I would get 15 per cent.

I agreed wholeheartedly with Damo's cut. He did the row, so he deserved the 60 per cent, if not more, but I wasn't doing it for 15 per cent if MacDara was getting 25 per cent. I had been such a yes-man throughout that project, they were taken aback when I didn't agree. They told me they needed an answer quickly and my reaction wasn't in the spirit of Project Empower. I was raging. It felt like I'd been blindsided. I told them that I didn't need to be part of the show, and it was only then that they told me they needed me. I was fuming. To cut a long story short, they came back with another offer that would have left me even worse off, but in the end it was Damo, not MacDara, who took the biggest cut to give me a share of 22.5 per cent, and that's not what I felt should have happened.

My feelings about the entire experience continued to be in turmoil. I have always loved, and thrived, being part of a team. On a team everyone's work has value, and everyone should feel like they are of value. On Project Empower I didn't. However, I do believe Damo was trying to be what he saw as a good leader, and I was still so grateful for the faith he had shown in me to ask me on the row, the opportunity he had given me.

The show was called *112 Days*, because that's how long Damo was at sea, and we sold out three nights in January 2023. It was really well put together, with Tomek's help. A lot of it was like a fireside chat, with MacDara sitting in a chair and interviewing first me, and then Damo. Even though I was only a small part of the show I really enjoyed both doing it and then talking to people afterwards. And that's when a lot of people started realising about my journey for the first time, that I had been paralysed from the waist down. So the show opened up a new window for me. People started asking me to talk at schools, and I realised I loved doing that, and it felt like I was making an impact. I was getting great reviews and teachers were rebooking me.

A few months later we got to see Tomek's documentary, *112 Days: Man vs Ocean*. There was a special screening at the Pálás Cinema for family and friends. It was a great day. Bradley, Felim and I had gone out to Inisheer, where I had been invited to open their annual 5k and 10k fundraising races. We were flown in and out, and then changed into smart clothes at the airport to rush back into the screening. I was sitting beside Damo and our families were all around us. Both of us got emotional as we watched. I could feel my internal reaction welling up when it came to the rescue, but it was even stronger when I talked about not wanting to be here any more, especially knowing my kids were seeing that too. At the time I was at my lowest they wouldn't have known anything. Mandy had protected them, and I am so grateful to her for that.

I had thought Damo getting back into Galway would allow me to finish the project in my head, even though it had ended for me a long time before that. While he was still rowing across that ocean it wasn't over. But I couldn't seem to let things go.

I took the anti-depressants for about six months, but decided it was time to get off them, and see where I was. I told Philip I wasn't comfortable staying on them, as I felt, like OxyNorm, they messed with my head. I felt calmer and more relaxed on them, but also a bit spaced-out, like I wasn't the same person; I wasn't me. I thought I was doing ok, but I was still very volatile, for no reason. It was like a switch would just go. I had tried online counselling while Damo was still at sea, but that didn't work. I was trying to do small tasks to keep me occupied. I did Coldtober, cold water immersion every day for a month, as an ambassador for Helplink Mental Health Services, which provides free and low-cost counselling services. But even if something worked for a little while I would find myself down that dark hole again. All the demons were still there, still gnawing away at me.

YOU WILL FACE SETBACKS.

You can't control everything. You can't fix everything.

26

TALKING A NEW PATH

Despite everything I had been through mentally and emotionally, even at this stage I still hadn't really asked for the one thing I needed most – help. I didn't even understand that I needed to ask for it.

I was sleeping really badly, waking up in a lather of sweat. I didn't want to see anybody or talk to anybody. I just wanted to be left alone. I just stayed at home. Normally I would be a tidiness freak. I have a place for everything. I couldn't sit down and watch TV or read a book if there were cups or plates to clear away. But during this period, the place was a mess, I let dishes pile up. Even opening my laptop was a mission. I just wasn't in a good place, and I knew it.

So finally I went back to Philip and told him I wasn't good and he suggested I try counselling with a psychologist or psychotherapist. He gave me a few numbers and I started making phone calls. That's how I found Ann Kelly at ProConsult, who was absolutely phenomenal. Meeting her and committing to therapy was my gamechanger. Since returning from the row, every night I would soak the bed in sweat. No matter what, I'd wake up and the bed would be soaked. I had told Ann about this. We had been talking for a while, getting into deeper stuff, and I think it was on my fifth or sixth visit that she mentioned something. A wave of relaxation came over my whole body, my face relaxed, my shoulders dropped. It was like I had been given a shot of morphine, and she said, 'We've got you!'

It was something back in my childhood that triggered that response. It was nothing particularly bad, but something, way back, that had made me feel I wasn't good enough. Ann explained to me, 'You're now listening to your inner child, the inner child that you have been fighting.' That's what had been coming out. When I felt like I was being attacked, or that somebody was doubting me, or somebody said I didn't do a job properly, I would hear that as 'You're not good enough.' If somebody had any negative comments at all, straight away it led me to think I was not good enough. That's what my inner child was hearing. My inner child believed that I had to leave the row because I was not good enough. My body had failed because I was not good enough. My marriage failed because I was not good enough. My business failed because I was not good enough. I woke the following morning and the sheets were dry, and I've never had night sweats since.

I now realise that I had used that feeling of not being good enough to propel myself through life, using it almost as a positive force. I had constantly used other people's negative comments as my fuel, driving me to prove them wrong. However, when the sense of failure became overwhelming it had broken me down.

Ann believed that my diaphragm and oesophagus were tensed up during the day, with the anxiety of holding that angry child in. This had come to the forefront after my accident, and had increased in New York, and then again after the row. What was happening at night was my body would relax and sweat it all out. My outbursts and occasional volatile explosions were because that angry inner child just needed to be heard. And every day I was starting the whole process again of bottling up that anger. All I was hearing was negativity. All I was feeling was depression. And I think that was why I developed massive anxiety in New York, and in the cabin on the boat, and I just couldn't get out of it.

Ann told me that I was now able to listen to my inner child, so I would no longer feel I had to hold anything back. I finally realised I needed to get rid of all the anger I had bottled up. It was the anger that was holding me back. Once I realised that, and took ownership of it, everything started changing. When you are positive, things start to fall into place more easily.

When I give talks now, one of my key messages is: 'There is amazing help out there, but you have to be the first person to put your hand up and say you need it.' I knew I needed it, but I had to go and ask for help. I was lucky I had Philip, my doctor, to guide me, and to encourage me to try one way, and when that didn't work to try another, and we eventually got to the right solution. You would be amazed at who will be there for you when you need them most. The services are there, and your friends and family are there, but you have to be brave and smart and strong enough to put your hand up and say you need help.

My learning curve from that whole experience was an understanding of why mental health issues and suicide rates are so high among men. We find it incredibly difficult to let the mask of masculinity down. We feel we are meant to be a provider, a keeper, a protector, a fixer, a human machine that just gets up and gets on with it; that is unbreakable. That is what I believed a man is meant to be. I had always fought against looking for help. Like many men, I thought 'I can fix this.' I always thought, I'll get it done myself. I'll do it my way. I felt like it would be another failure if I asked for help. But ultimately, there are times in your life you have to be courageous enough to raise your hand and look for the help you need.

The help I got showed me that two of the things that really affect my mental health are loneliness and failure. I'm able to deal with them better now, thanks to Ann. I know criticism is not a personal attack, or that it's a failure, it's just the way I perceive it. Then when I started looking back at my own personal journey with a new perspective, I gradually came to the understanding, the realisation, that I had been very hard on myself. I had been frustrated at how I had lost my energy; despite all the rowing and gruelling fitness training, I thought I had my body and mindset prepared, everything boxed off to take on the challenge of the row. I realised now that what I hadn't had was the bodily resilience the row required.

COVID and other factors had kept throwing up obstacles, preventing us from preparing as planned. However, Damo had rowed an ocean before. He knew what it was like to be out in an ocean, but he had also built up a massive resilience in his body from all his other endeavours and challenges. He has constantly challenged his body for decades, attempting to climb Everest and ultimately the Seven Summits, the ultra marathons. No training could substitute for the resilience that he has built into his body, from all his ordeals, all his endeavours, from everything he has pitted his body, and mind, against. He was a trained elite athlete. I was coming from a bed, from having a spinal cord injury, to attempting one of the biggest challenges a person could possibly take on. I just assumed that because of what I had come through, and because I felt very strong, I would prevail. But I really didn't understand the hardship my body would face. I had walked across the country, but I had slept in hotels every night. I had trained hard for the row in the gym, but I still slept every night in my own bed and ate home-cooked food.

Perhaps if I had had the time to complete other smaller challenges my body would not have let me down. If the pandemic hadn't happened; if our training had gone as planned; if I had had a chance to get used to life on an ocean rowing boat; if my body had been better prepared there might have been a different outcome. I'll never know. But now I finally accepted that my body had given up because I hadn't prepared it right. It wasn't that I hadn't tried hard enough.

It's possible that trying too hard, that huge exertion to get into the Gulf Stream, also took its toll on my body and played into my downfall. We were determined to just keep going, no matter how tired we were, no matter what the weather or the wave conditions. We got up, we got on the saddle, and we rowed. That constant push onwards may have been one of the factors that led to me having to be extracted, even though the rowing was far easier at that stage. I believe that when an opportunity presents itself, you just have to go for it. Damo had given me, a simple man from Galway, the opportunity of a lifetime to try and do something extraordinary. I had jumped, but in hindsight I wondered if I jumped in a little too soon.

Finally, as I began looking at things in a more positive light, I started allowing myself to feel pride in what I had done. I had only lasted 13 days, but I could take pride in what I had achieved. For so long, when I thought about Project Empower, I could only think about being told I was finished, being taken off the *Cushlamachree*, hiding away from everyone, ruminating about the training and preparation. I am now a firm believer that you look at the journey, not the ending, and what a journey it was. Now when I think about Project Empower I think about it positively. I think of how I started with five minutes on the rowing machine and then completed the equivalent of seven marathons in seven days. I think of rowing a currach, of watching *Cushlamachree* take shape, and all the fantastic people I met along the way.

Now I look at what I achieved. It made me fitter. It helped my progress in terms of my disability. From the moment I took on that row, I enjoyed some incredible experiences. I was so lucky in so many ways, and I have Damo to thank for that. In my wildest dreams, even before my accident, I would never have imagined rowing around the Statue of Liberty, giving a talk in the New York Athletic Club, being on NBC News. There were so many unique, unrepeatable standout moments. How many people will ever get to row out of Manhattan with the city lights behind them; be head-butted by flying fish; or swim in the Gulf Stream?

It's a chapter that I'm absolutely delighted was included in my life, that I'm grateful for, but also glad it is now closed. A lot of my anger had been directed towards others, at what I perceived as injustices – even though some of them weren't – but now that I had let go of that anger I could focus again on the future.

I hope Damo and I will always be friends, but I don't think our relationship will ever be the same again. Some of our issues were definitely down to communication, and I now appreciate that we are all different and we all think differently. He would certainly have a very different viewpoint and perspective from mine on a lot of things that happened, and I understand that now. If he called me right now and asked for help I would drop everything and go. We were also on different paths, with different things driving us. My path was not a chosen one. It was ordained by my accident. I discovered by default that I really like challenges. Damo's is the path he has chosen, and he's very driven to take on challenges and very focused on what he wants to achieve.

Project Empower took me to the depths of despair, but it raised a lot of money for charity – almost €77,000 – gave me so much to be grateful for and opened up a new world for me, a new career path.

I'm slowly building up a business giving motivational talks, as well as speaking about health and safety, and mental health issues. I've created a website, but most of my talks are booked through word of mouth, so it is obviously hitting home with people. I have spoken in front of a huge variety of people, including construction workers, students, health workers, fellow spinal injury patients. I am proud to say that I am now an ambassador for the Lighthouse Charity and their Make it Visible initiative. It is an amazing organisation that helps construction workers and their families in times of crisis. I am constantly inspired by organisations like Active Disability Ireland, the NRH Foundation and Spinal Injuries Ireland, and their work to make Ireland inclusive for all.

I am progressing all the time, I am changing all the time. So none of my talks is exactly the same. I make new realisations constantly, and learn new things about myself and what is important. I now see the world from different viewpoints. I love sharing my unique life story, the story of my physical and mental struggles, especially when people approach me afterwards to tell me it has made them think deeply about their own lives. Health and safety begins long before you walk through the doors at work. Sharing the story of my own workplace accident and all the mental and emotional hardships that my family, business and friends had to endure while I was making a recovery really seems to hit home, illustrating how something as simple as one workplace mistake can have dire consequences.

After the row, Fernanda and I continued to see each other on and off for a long time. At one time the plan was that she would move to Ireland to be with me every second week. She is an amazing woman, but we started getting annoyed with each other a lot. We would argue and neither of us would be willing to concede. We are too alike in many ways. We had begun a business together, doing bus tours for Portuguese and Spanish speakers, but it was an ill-conceived idea. We didn't work well together, and it created conflict between us. Then it started affecting time with my kids, and that had been my red line, so it ultimately drove us further apart. We went our separate ways in early 2024. I was very sad when it was over, but it was for the best, and I moved on to the next part of my journey.

ASK FOR AND TAKE THE HELP YOU NEED. YOU ARE GOOD ENOUGH. LET GO OF THE ANGER.

Asking for help was the most powerful and important thing I did on my road to recovery. It was only when I talked and shared my worries, and said I needed help, that I realised how much support I had around me, and available to me. I had just needed to put up my hand and ask. When we neglect our mental health everyone around us also suffers. Asking for help is a sign of strength, not a sign of weakness.

27

OTHER CHALLENGES

In February 2023 I ticked another achievement off the mental bucket list I had made when I left the NRH by climbing Carrauntoohil, the highest peak in Ireland, with my friend Christian Short. For months I hadn't been feeling great, I had lost my zest for life, but that day gave me a great lift. I felt afraid coming down the Devil's Ladder. Going up was fine, but when you don't have proprioception you have to have two points of contact at all times. It's easy going up because you put your hand in front of you and there's solid rock to hold on to, but coming down there is nothing in front. You have to put your hand on the ground behind you, and only then can you lift your foot, so you are coming down on your arse. I know my limitations, so it was scary. Despite that, it was a thrill. I loved it because climbing mountains is hard. Unlike walking, it gets your heart pumping, it gets you sweating, and it brings an incredible sense of achievement. I would urge everyone who can do it to get out on a mountain, to do it while you can. Don't take your ability to climb a hill or a mountain for granted. Do it now.

However, the sense of failure continued to dog me. Counselling was starting to really help me, and I knew I needed to reset my mind. I decided it was time to challenge myself again. I needed to feel that sense of accomplishment I had experienced after the walk in 2019, after rowing in a currach from the Aran Islands. I believed that doing something difficult would finally give me the sense of accomplishment that I craved, and would raise more money for the NRH.

I had started doing an occasional bit of bus driving again, and I was in Kerry with some Swedish tourists. The first night I was in Tralee at the Brandon Hotel, I recorded a second 'What Makes You Tick' podcast with Stephen Bradshaw, where he questioned if I was ever kind to myself. The next day, as I drove around the Dingle Peninsula, I began to think about things, about where I was at in my own head. That evening, when I got back to the hotel, I put on my training gear and decided to run out towards Blennerville. I thought I might make it to the windmill, but I ran past it, and I kept going.

I had never tried to run any sort of distance since my accident, because it felt so strange. As I don't have sensation in my feet, I don't feel impact from the road. I feel it in my knees, in my hips. It's a very weird sensation. In addition, because I don't have proprioception, when my feet are airborne I actually don't know where they are. It's impossible to describe what that feels like. Running wasn't a comfortable thing to do; it was very unsettling. So I decided it was time to run more!

I decided that, to mark the fifth anniversary of leaving the NRH, I would run across the country from our yard to the hospital doors. I would run 208km over four days, 52km a day, the equivalent of around five marathons. My friend Robbie Kavanagh decided to join me. I had played Connacht juniors rugby with Robbie, and he had played with Monivea as well. We hadn't seen each other for a long time when I met him again by chance. I was dropping Aimee off to soccer trials in Galway and his daughter was also trying out.

I told him about the challenge I was planning, and he asked if anyone was joining me. I told him no. The next day he rang me to say that he would run with me, that it was exactly what he needed as he was struggling with severe rheumatoid arthritis, which was very debilitating. We had the same mindset – to push ourselves.

I had never attempted to run a marathon, even when I was fully able-bodied. I never even tried to run for a long time after my accident, because I didn't know I could. I had tried CrossFit, but I always struggled with the parts where there's a lot of body movement. CrossFit is very much a team sport and I was getting frustrated because even on my third event I wasn't finding it easier. I was able to catch up on the rowing and the cycle, but my body wasn't trained for the running, or the body weight movements.

Even setting that challenge, deciding I was going to do it, lifted my spirits, and the endorphins kicked in when I started training. I now had something to focus on every evening, rather than sitting home and doing nothing. There was an immediate sense of satisfaction. I could feel my energy returning. This was a difficult challenge, but one that was in my control, that I felt I could complete. I could have run one marathon, but I didn't think that was difficult enough. I wanted to put more pressure on myself. I wanted to put myself through pain. I wanted to put myself into doubt. However, I knew it was doable. Unlike the row, I would sleep in a bed every night. I would have access to good food. I could have daily ice baths and physiotherapy if I needed it.

My kids were so proud that I was taking on another challenge. I told my young ladeen a few weeks before I told anybody else and he came to do little jogs with me down the boreen, just to do the training with me. I felt that I was showing them once again that if you want to do something it's within you if you get up off your backside, and don't wait for somebody to do it for you. Having challenges in front of me sharpens my mind and gets me up and moving on the days when I am feeling lazy or lethargic. When I set myself a challenge and put it out there, there's no hiding!

When I train I visualise. I visualise my feet making contact with the ground. I visualise what I will do when I reach a hill and more effort will be needed. I visualise the finish line. I probably ran about 8km that first night in Kerry, and gradually increased the distance. When I reached 15km I got ultra-runner Conor O'Keefe involved. He actually advised me I was overloading myself too quickly and he brought down the numbers.

As usual I loved the routine and the effort that training brought, and it even delivered a very magical moment. One evening, after driving a bus, I found myself in a hotel in Cavan overlooking lakes. It was windy and the roads were dark and surrounded by trees. I put on my gear and took off running. I had no idea where I was going but decided I would run for as long as I could. As I ran down by the lake, my mind suddenly focused in on the nature around me. I could hear the pounding of my feet, the wind, the birds – mainly crows cawing – the lapping of the water in the lake. I felt immersed in nature and the positive feeling that gave me blew me away. I had so much positive energy I could have stayed running all night. I wasn't even noticing my legs moving. It was just a surreal and special episode.

Now, looking back, I remember that when I was younger, to get fit I would get up in the dark before school, about 5.30 or 6 a.m., and run a five-mile loop from my house. Part of that run was past a forest, and maybe that moment in Cavan was triggering a memory for me, the dark, the trees, the sounds. However, whatever the reason I had that serene experience, it made me realise how important being out in nature is for my wellbeing, and what positive energy Mother Nature can supply.

In September 2023 I announced the challenge:

> It's been a very difficult year for me mentally, emotionally, and physically. I was in a very negative place without realising it. I was not a good person to be around to tell the truth, I was so negative to be around.
>
> Thankfully, with the help of my friends, family, and therapy I now have my mojo back and raring to go again and inspire people to follow their dreams and encourage people to have a never say never attitude.

Conor gave us a strategy for the five days; how not to overload ourselves and when to walk to give our bodies a break – how to pace ourselves. We didn't give ourselves a huge amount of time for training and the furthest distance I ran before we set off was about 22km. I also wanted to show that I could push myself to achieve our goal without training fully; this would be pre-planned but not fully prepared. I would have to dig deep every day, and that is what I wanted. That's where the biggest challenge would be; when my body was saying no, and everything around me was saying no, to keep my mind positive, push beyond the pain barrier, and get myself over the line.

Robbie and I completed that run, with Willie Parker in our support car. We were welcomed back through the doors of the NRH on 26 October 2023 and raised almost €9,000 for the NRH. We were both in bits. Like everything else I do, I used pure motor mechanics to propel my lower body. I didn't feel its impact really in my feet, but it had a huge impact elsewhere. My hip was on fire despite all the drugs I take to mask pain. I had the left hip resurfaced years ago and that was on the way out, and the right hip needed replacing, even before the accident. I finally got a new hip in March 2025.

I probably shouldn't have taken on those runs, because it brought on a lot of extra suffering and pain, but I wanted to prove once again that if I put my mind to something I could do it. I won't run again though. That was the end of distance running for me, though I made an exception for Aimee, running with her for her first Fields of Athenry 10k that December. I was incredibly proud of her.

I was still drawn to mountain challenges, though, and so was my running mate Robbie. To raise money for Ability West and AsIAm Ireland, we planned to do the Four Peaks Challenge – climbing the highest peaks in each province within 24 hours, driving between each mountain. Unfortunately I had to pull out. I had completed three of the peaks separately: Mweelrea (814m), Carrauntoohil (1038m) and Slieve Donard (850m). But after Slieve Donard I was so crippled that I had to concede I would not be able to do them all in 24 hours. That was disappointing. Instead I drove Robbie between mountains. He smashed the challenge and it raised €26,000.

At another stage, after leaving the NRH, I had an opportunity to try out for the Paralympics in different events for 2024. Discus and shotput were considered my best options. I trained for about three months, but then realised I wasn't enjoying the solitary nature of the sport, and my hips were acting up. They wouldn't have endured the training required to qualify for Paralympic competition. I did get to go to the Paralympics, but as an observer, as a guest of Toyota Ireland. It was a fantastic experience to get to the Stade de France, to have lunch in the Versailles Palace, to meet inspirational athletes like Ellen Keane and Olympian David Gillick, and to watch the action. I also got to visit a mobility park built by Toyota for the event, which showed what's possible, and set the standard for any country trying to do what is best for its disabled citizens: mobility is inclusivity. My heart was full as I headed home after watching the games. However, not once during that trip had I felt I was missing out by being just an observer, that I should have been there as an athlete. Being a Paralympian was not destined to be part of my own journey.

Paralympic athletes are real heroes. They face their challenges daily without complaint and show us what true perseverance looks like. The effort they put in to compete, to excel, is phenomenal, and it begins long before they start their training. Able-bodied people have no conception of how long it can take to shower, dress or get ready if you are a wheelchair user, a blade wearer, or profoundly visually impaired. Almost every mundane task is more difficult, requiring greater effort and time.

Through my own journey, I had some understanding of the immense effort and commitment Paralympic athletes pour into their sport, their training. We can all be inspired. Every one of us faces challenges or can set themselves challenges. They are not just the walks and the rows and the runs, or the bids for gold medals. A challenge can be physical or mental or emotional, as long as it is something that will improve you, and keep your mind in the present rather than the past.

When I left the NRH I vowed to raise €250,000 for charity, but I also keep doing challenges because it keeps me fit, keeps me focused, keeps me moving forward. I don't ever want to let myself get back into my comfort zone ever again. I'm actually afraid to let myself back into that comfort zone, because I don't know how I would react, how easily I could get myself back out of it. I am afraid I will start getting weaker on my feet and start losing my balance more easily again. I don't want to find out what the physical and mental health repercussions would be, so I keep training, keep pushing myself.

Before the accident I was working 24/7, eating rubbish, not exercising, not caring about the effects on my health. Having a spinal cord injury lowers your life expectancy, and while I don't think about that reality too often, that fact does stop me letting myself off the hook or falling back into bad habits, and keeps me challenging myself.

EVERY DAY IS A DAY TO IMPROVE.

This remains my mantra. Every day is also a new day, a fresh chance to start over. There are so many different ways you can improve every day, physically, mentally, emotionally and educationally.

I believe recovery from any accident or injury never stops. It's the person that stops. We all have good days and bad days, but we need to keep pushing ourselves, to take on new challenges.

28

HOW AM I NOW?

I know I am in a very lucky position. I was a completely independent person, the provider for a lot of people. Then, in an instant, I was completely dependent. I relied on everybody and anybody around me. And then, when I was trying to regain some independence, my business and relationships failed. So as I was trying to become independent again, I wasn't a provider any more, and that played hell with my head. But I'm very lucky that I'm independent again. So I know what it's like for somebody in three life situations: being completely independent; being completely dependent; and having a hidden disability.

It is a hidden disability that can impact my personal dignity, my personal pride. People are constantly asking me, 'How's your back?' But my back is fine after the operation. That's not the problem. People see me, and say, 'Oh, you're doing so well. You're looking great. You're looking stronger, better than ever before.' And physically, parts of that are true. But as I'm listening to them I'm constantly moving my toes and my feet, trying to keep the pain at bay.

Even people who know me well still forget about my disability. One evening while I was recovering from my hip replacement – which was far more difficult than I had expected – I dozed off on the couch. Aimee was trying to wake me up and she was tapping my legs for ages before she remembered that I couldn't feel that tapping, that I had no sensation. It was her laughter that woke me up, she was laughing that she had forgotten, and had been hammering away at my legs.

There's a belief that because I beat the prognosis of never walking again that I can do everything, but I can't. Even when you try to explain to people you know it goes over their heads. Their focus is on your feet, and once they see them on the ground, they think everything is back in working order. I'm a big, strong man, and nobody understands those hidden issues – the pain, the lack of proprioception, the lack of control over my bodily functions, the exhaustion. When I'm sick, even with a cold, I second-guess why I'm sick, or why I've got sick. Did I overdo it? Or is this my condition getting worse?

I would never wish myself back into a wheelchair. I am so grateful that I don't need one, but sometimes I think that if I was in a wheelchair I wouldn't have to deal with all the questions, and being told that I'm 'flying it'. It can be so wearing trying to get people to understand I still live with consequences of my accident, every second of every day. Even now when I'm going up a staircase, I have to put my hand on the rail to keep my balance. I have such reduced feeling and sensation from my belly button down that I could be playing footsie with somebody underneath the table and not know it!

So what can I feel on my legs? A soft touch, like a caress, or a feather being run along my skin, will give me a tingling sensation; but if you walloped my thigh or my calf I'd feel nothing. I can't feel my arse. I spent hours one day in a hotel thinking I'd lost my phone, or it had been stolen, but it was in my back pocket the whole time. I got everyone looking for it. I don't know what eventually made me feel my backside with my hand and it was there. I can wear shorts now even in the coldest weather. I won't feel the cold or the breeze, even though the hair on my legs will be standing up. I'll start to feel cold up around my trunk long before I feel it on my legs. Even if you put an ice-pack on them I wouldn't feel it for quite a while. What I feel doesn't make sense.

My internal thermometer seems to be all over the place. I can sweat an awful lot when I exercise, but one day I'll be sweating doing the slightest exertion, and another day not a drop. The body isn't talking to itself properly. Sometimes on the coldest of nights I'll be roasting, sleeping with just a sheet over me.

Up in the top few inches of my head I believe I can still do everything. So I try to still do everything and sometimes that doesn't go well. After Storm Éowyn in early 2025 I was cutting trees with a chainsaw and I fell. I fell because, even though I'm moving them, I don't have feelings in my legs. Cutting trees with a chainsaw is harder because I don't have my balance, and I have to get myself into certain positions to manage it. But that's all kind of inbuilt now. I know how to adjust myself, to adjust how I'm standing. However I need to be extra cautious, which I forget at times. So when I was cutting the trees some branches had fallen behind the back of my legs, but I didn't feel them. Then when I went to move back I fell over. I fell back, and when I was falling, I hit off something else, and the chainsaw hit my knee. Thankfully it bounced off the knee and fell away. I only needed a few stitches.

I can't throw my leg over anything. I can't climb over anything. I can't climb up things – I can't go up and down ladders. I find negotiating stairs difficult. There are so many different things I'm not able to do. I can't stand on one leg for more than a few seconds without falling over. If I close my eyes I'll fall over instantly if I'm not touching something, like a wall.

But I'm upright, and I'm walking. I can do 95 per cent of what everybody else does, though I look very awkward in certain situations. I go to the gym four days a week minimum, and I'm as strong and as fit as anybody there for my age, probably stronger than a lot of men younger than me. I can do everything in the gym in terms of weights or machine weights, where your feet are planted. However, I don't do exercises like burpees any more because I can't see my feet. When I can't see my feet, or when they are not in contact with the ground or surface, I struggle. When my legs are dangling I don't know where they are.

And if you asked me to lift something, or run in an everyday scenario, I have to think about it. I have to make sure that my body is in a certain position so I don't fall over. I can't react to anything quickly, and that continuous thinking about my next move is exhausting. That's something that people just don't see and don't understand. Everything I do now is almost robotic, as it is trained into my systems. Whereas if I have to do something I haven't done before, like maybe bend over in a certain position, I lose all strength and fall over because I haven't trained that movement into me. That still happens frequently because I can't train for every movement. I slip a lot, and while most people might be able to stop themselves falling I'll be gone. I have to be particularly wary in showers I'm not used to.

I still do a lot of rowing, which is quite hard on my legs, and I do a lot of uphill walking in the gym, but I'd prefer to go off hiking, even though hiking is very difficult for me because of my lack of stability and proprioception. I drove a busload from a Tuam gym to Diamond Hill in Connemara last year, and I brought my shorts and T-shirt, because I thought I might do it, if it was a nice day. I parked up the bus and as they started heading off, I decided to go for it, as hard as I could. I threw on my shoes and shorts, and away I went, and I got up and down quicker than any of them on the bus, because I was flying fit at the time, but throughout the whole thing I wasn't able to enjoy the view. The competitive streak in me wouldn't have let me go up that hill if I didn't think I would do well. I did it in 51 minutes, but only because I had been doing a lot of hiking and mountaineering at that stage and my body was used to it. I had also been up and down Diamond Hill a good few times, so I knew where it would be tough. So I can do things; it just takes me longer to train up for them. If I went out to do a mountain today, even though I'm fit, it would probably take me a lot longer, because I haven't been doing as much hiking. Because my movement is so mechanical, it seems that I can only ever train for one discipline at a time.

Even though I know my own limitations, I still get annoyed if somebody who knows me tells me to take it easy, or says 'Maybe you shouldn't do that.' They may mean well, maybe they are saying it out of kindness, but that's not what I hear. I hear 'You can't do it.' I hate the word 'can't'. I hate hearing people use the word can't as an excuse not to get out of their comfort zone. That word sets me off. Don't start with the excuse. At least try. I couldn't walk, but if I had kept telling myself 'I can't' I would never have walked again.

However, there are things that I would love to be able to do but I have to accept I really can't, or I shouldn't. I would love to do more mountaineering, but I have to admit it's not in my capability to ever climb Everest or other peaks because I don't have the sensation in my feet to be able to go through ice, or to have the balance needed to descend.

I try not to think about my limitations or my hidden disabilities too much, because if I did my head would be melted. I just get on with it and keep myself occupied and as busy as possible. If you sit down and start thinking about all the stuff you can't do, or the difficulties you have to deal with, your head would be fried.

Pain has been a constant and unwelcome companion on my journey. Nerve pain remains the worst ongoing legacy of my accident. It's not the usual type of pain that many people will be familiar with. It feels like my feet are on fire. When the nerve pain is reduced, it's like the feet are on fire from the ankles down. But when the nerve pain increases, it travels up through my legs. The closest analogy I can think of is if you put your feet up beside a fire and the soles start getting roasting hot and you need to pull them back, but you can't. I don't have that luxury. And then as the fire gets hotter the heat travels up through my legs. That's what it's like – 24/7.

If I'm standing up talking to people I need to constantly move my weight from one foot to the other to suppress the pain a little. I don't even notice I'm doing it at this stage, it's just part of who I am. Nights are the worst, because once I take my feet off the ground, that pressure isn't going down through my legs, so the nerve pain increases. When I'm lying in bed, because I have no weight on them, and I can't see them under the blanket, I actually don't know where my feet are.

The pain fluctuates. Some days it's not so bad, other days it's through the roof, and there doesn't seem to be a reason why it's higher or lower. Some nights it will be so bad I won't sleep at all. That can happen if I overdo my training. That's probably my biggest weakness. I don't know when to take it easy, and that can increase the pain. Moderation has never really been in my DNA. However, there is no pattern. I could train very hard one day and sleep perfectly that night. I could train hard another day and the pain will be through the roof. Yesterday I was actually off my feet most of the day because I was in the car but the pain last night was excruciating.

I am still on a high dosage of gabapentin for nerve pain. It doesn't get rid of it, it just numbs or suppresses it, masks it a little. But even if I mightn't feel the pain as much because of the medication, my body is still fighting it, and that leads to a huge amount of fatigue. That fatigue, that exhaustion, can hit me like a ton of bricks out of nowhere. And that's hard, listening to my body and saying, 'Okay, I need to stop. I need to rest and recover.' I might need to rest for a day, just sit down and do nothing. It is very, very hard to get your mind around doing that when you are not that type of person. But I have to force myself to rest, or I will end up even sorer.

People often don't understand just how tired I can be, and I don't blame them. I wouldn't get it either. Sometimes I see my dad coming in to me, and I'm sitting down in the middle of the day watching TV, and I struggle to even have a conversation with him, and he tuts and goes out the door again. He's a man who got up every day of his life and got on with it and got things done. That's who he is, so he can't understand anyone who might be watching

TV in the middle of the day and not doing something. It's an extremely difficult thing for people to understand, because they just don't see my tiredness or understand why I can get grumpy or withdrawn. I don't understand it myself. I try not to let the pain get into my head, and the way I do that is to keep my mind occupied, distracted by other stuff.

Everything is a distraction for me, though sometimes that has been a bad thing, because instead of facing my problems I would distract myself from them. I am now better at facing problems head on, because I don't want them to stack up and add to the pile that are already there. I do things straight away. A bill? I'll pay it immediately. If something has to be done. I'll do it there and then. And this keeps the pressure off, because I can't deal with pressure any more.

How am I mentally? That's always a challenge. I can now recognise the signs that I'm going into a hole. If I'm not putting away a dirty cup, that's a sign I'm beginning to drift. If I try to avoid doing things, or keep to myself in a coffee shop, or avoid socialising, that's me beginning to drift. I need sleep, exercise, healthy food, to get outdoors into the fresh air, to have cold showers. These are all mandatory.

It's amazing how your mindset can change. Before the accident I would have driven and parked as close as possible to anywhere I was going, so I would have to walk as little as possible. Now, walking around Galway, out to Salthill, is nothing. I take every opportunity I can to exercise, to get fresh air.

I go to the gym. It keeps the weight down and I look a bit better, but I really go for the mental side of things – the workouts I do there definitely help me maintain my mental health – and the social side of things and the camaraderie. I don't have that team environment any more. I can't play team sports. If I could, I'd be down playing soccer, rather than being in the gym. One of my friends from the NRH has gone on to play wheelchair basketball for Ireland, and that's brilliant. He has asked me to go and play, and I would be eligible, but I just wouldn't feel comfortable standing up from my wheelchair after a game and walking away, when so many other people on the team can't. I still feel guilty that I am on my feet again, while so many others aren't. It's almost like I have 'imposter syndrome' about my spinal cord injury because I can now walk. I feel guilty that I'm so much better off than some of my friends from the NRH, and that guilt makes me interact less with them – and other people with paralysis – even though I'd like to be interacting more. I still feel guilt that I am back on my feet, and they are not.

If I have too much time to myself, if I don't keep myself occupied, I start going down the slippery slope. When we didn't have the power or water for a week after Storm Éowyn I found myself eating badly and not sleeping well, even though we were going to bed early. I couldn't shower. I couldn't do what usually keeps me well. I wasn't able to exercise either, aside from walking. I missed both the exercise and the social side of going to the gym, because you'll always have a chat with someone. Walking on your own isn't very social. We didn't even have the internet for a couple of days, so that challenged me mentally. I could feel myself getting lower and lower. But thankfully now I know the tools to get out of that. The minute the electricity was back I had a shower – a hot one first, which was lovely, and then a cold one!

Keeping my mind occupied and myself distracted also prevents me feeling lonely, which is still something that can get in on me. If I am feeling lonely then I will start feeling sad, and then I might get upset and start overthinking about things that have happened in recent years, about mistakes I have made, about what I should or could have done, about how I'm not in the house I built with my family – even though I know all this is pointless.

I'm also now beginning to understand how that fear of loneliness has affected my life in other ways. I've been working with a dietician recently and he has been talking to me about why I eat, rather than just what I eat. So when I am sitting watching TV, and I'm not fully immersed in what's on, I might start feeling lonely, and that feels uncomfortable. So to comfort myself I make a cup of tea and eat a few biscuits. He's suggesting I learn to sit with that feeling of discomfort for half an hour. And then after half an hour I might still make that cup of tea, but I mightn't reach for chocolate or biscuits or something to eat that isn't going to serve me; that I was only reaching for as a way to soothe myself. Sometimes it works and sometimes it doesn't.

I love having the kids around more in the summer, and I have dogs and cats to keep me busy when they're not with me. Having dogs and cats in my home and life is more important to me now than ever. They are a huge comfort and help prevent me getting lonely. The kids all help mind my pets when I am away. I think pets have always helped anchor them too and helped them to manage difficult transitions, including when I am away for a while.

Challenges like the row, and the trans-America walk I'm planning for 2026, take me away from them but I think they understand, and I think they are proud of me. The row made the 9 o'clock NBC news in America just before we left New York. I had kept a recording and Bradley and I watched it recently together. Afterwards he gave me a huge hug. I know he's proud of me.

I realised recently how much my mindset has changed. I remembered a conversation I had years ago on a night out with a good friend who had recently lost his father to cancer. He was talking about how he had no proper memories of his father, or time spent with him, because his father was always working. I kept telling him, 'Your dad worked hard to give you the life you have now.' That's what my take was, and I kept arguing with him, insisting that his father had been working to give him a good life. My friend understood that, but he said, 'What good is that to me? I don't have any of the memories you should have of your father.'

I couldn't see where he was coming from then, but now I do. My whole life was all about working hard, making money and growing a business. Now I can absolutely see his point, and that's why creating memories for my kids is one of my greatest priorities. At that time, I thought he was completely wrong. Now I realise how right he was. That friend got what was important, way before I did.

I was good with the kids before the accident, but I saw myself as the provider, the fixer who had to keep his head down and work hard so my family could have a good life. My kids have taught me that our children just want to spend time with us, no matter what we are doing. When I taught Bradley how to make a cup of tea, all he wanted to do was make me tea and toast. Felim doesn't stop from morning until night. He's a handful. He could get in and start up a coach at five years of age, so you have to keep an eye on him all the time. But he just wants to be doing things with me, to help me. Aimee, even though she is a teenager, loves having the chats, and I really treasure that. Everything I tell her is wrong, of course, the way I thought everything my parents told me was wrong, but that makes me laugh.

I love spending time with them. When they are growing up your children just want to be around you. But they want to be around you when you are being a good person, and that's what I'm trying to be.

MAKE MEMORIES WITH THOSE YOU LOVE.

My kids have taught me that our children just want to spend time with us, with the best version of us. Shared experiences are what bring us together with our families and friends, what can bring us the most joy, and give us those special standout moments in our lives.

29

REBUILDING A BETTER MAN

Earlier this year I rebuilt a drystone wall on my father's land. I rebuilt it with my bare hands because I could. I felt very lucky and privileged to be able to do it, that I was now physically able to complete the task – knowing so many people aren't – and that I had the luxury of time to do it.

Building a stone wall takes time, and some heavy lifting. It began to symbolise two things to me, both the physical rebuilding that so many people with a disability or illness have to face, but it also a metaphor for the wall people with mental health issues have to overcome.

It is good for the head to do a job like that, one that is long-lasting, that you can see take shape in front of you. It's an accomplishment. I earn huge satisfaction from undertaking a project like that and doing it right. Now more than ever I know the value of doing things properly; even if it takes me a month to complete a task I'd prefer to do it carefully and correctly.

Like so many other people in this world, my life changed in the blink of an eye and I had to adapt. Since that day I have learned that, like a stone wall, when your life collapses, or your body or mind collapses, it can be rebuilt. But it has to be done correctly. You have to build a strong foundation and place every stone carefully, or it will collapse again. Like my own rebuilding, I had to remove and redo or replace sections that weren't sitting right or holding steady as I went along. Rebuilding myself has taken time, and some heavy lifting, and it hasn't been as easy or as enjoyable as those February days I spent outdoors rebuilding that wall.

I realise now that 26 October 2018 was both the worst and greatest day of my life. I made a huge mistake when I picked up that rusty bench in my work yard. However, that mistake turned out to be a blessing, a gift to myself, to a man who had lost his way. It forced me to change how I looked at life. I've had two lives, really, my life up to the point where I had my accident, and my life afterwards. That first life was filled with stress, worry and debt. I was overweight and unhealthy. My pursuit of success had turned me from an optimistic, energetic and loving young man into a completely different animal, a sometimes selfish animal. I was so focused on being successful, in making a business that the world would see as a success, that I let everything else take second place, including my relationships with my wife and children. Underneath I was a narky, sharp-tongued, unhappy person. When the accident happened I had no relationship with my baby son, and that was a decision I had made. I had let that happen.

After the accident, with a broken body, business and marriage, I felt like a shell of a man. It took me a long time to finally understand that the shell was probably still a better man than I had been. My accident was a turning point, the start of my second life. It spurred me to rebuild myself into a fitter person, a healthier person and, I hope, a better person. But it didn't just happen. I had to work hard at it. I'm still working at it. Having a spinal cord injury has actually changed my life for the better. I've lived a life since that day that I couldn't ever have imagined.

But my journey has not been a solo one. I have so much to thank others for: my family, my friends, my colleagues, and of course the staff at the Mater Spinal Injuries Unit, St Finbar's Orthopaedic Ward, and the National Rehabilitation Hospital.

I was told I would never walk again. However, I chose not to accept that prognosis, and I would eventually defy the odds that were against me. However, it has been the toughest trek.

Along the way I've learned to collect the building blocks and the tools I've needed. Some of these have included stubbornness, hard work, positivity (and negativity), finding inspiration, gruelling training regimes, gentle exercise, perseverance, understanding, rest, therapy, gratitude and friendships.

Resilience is a word that gets used a lot these days, but where I come from in County Galway the word we use more often is 'thick'. Thickness to me is a stubbornness that stops you giving in, an understanding that you have to dig in and work harder so you don't budge, don't give way. It's being 'pure thick' that kept me going, against the odds. It's that trait of 'thickness' that kept me going on the rugby field, kept me bulling ahead in business, and would eventually stop me accepting a prognosis that would keep me in a wheelchair for the rest of my life.

I have repeatedly ignored any prognosis I have been given. I was told that progress from a spinal injury usually stalls after one year, but I wasn't going to accept that. The difference between how I walk now and how I walked a year after leaving the NRH is remarkable. I don't understand why those limits are set, or why people are given those limits and accept them. Maybe it's just my mindset, but I can't understand why other people don't see it the way I do.

Even on my worst days I still looked for a physical improvement, because it was something I could control.

People like to stay in their comfort zones, they don't like being pushed. Physically I didn't need anyone to push me on my rehabilitation journey; I push myself. However, I needed that pushback when I was playing rugby and soccer. I needed the negativity of someone telling me I was useless to keep driving me to run more sprints back to back, or train harder. I still talk negatively to myself, berating myself when I'm not up to par, to make myself do better, to motivate me to get on with something. I'm not sure what a psychologist would think of that. I still think about that question Stephen Bradshaw asked me on his podcast *What Makes You Tick*: Fergus, are you ever kind to yourself? Maybe I'm not as kind as I should be to myself, but that is just not the way I'm geared. I thrive on other people's negativity, on being told I can't do something. If somebody says I can't do something, it'll make me try and do it. And I think sometimes I have to also be negative to myself, in order to push myself. I think that's just ingrained in me. Maybe I feel if I am kind to myself I will get lazy.

When something as traumatic as a spinal cord injury happens to you, and you are the only person who can get yourself out of it, I struggle with how someone can adopt a mindset of, 'Okay, so that's it for me.' I struggle with understanding how you wouldn't want to improve your life, even in the smallest way. I found inspiration to improve all around me, most often from other spinal cord injury patients.

Physically I am still constantly rebuilding my body. When I stop training, I go backwards because I don't have proprioception. My core weakens because of that lack of feeling, of sensation. I fall over more easily. Training, for me, is imperative, not just as a therapy, but to keep me upright and moving.

I am now healthier overall. Before the accident I was obese. I was less flexible. My body was under pressure all the time. I was fatigued. My sleep was poor, and broken. I had become so deeply unhealthy that I didn't even realise how bad I was. Now I know that if I don't give myself the right nutrition, if I go a few days without exercising properly, I quickly feel a mental deterioration. I do feel fitter and healthier when my weight is down. I am not a nutritionist or a health expert, but when I'm a certain weight, 105kg rather than 110kg, I feel better. Those kilos are an indicator to me that things are going the right or the wrong way. And when I feel better I train harder and I eat more healthily. If I'm at home I have two dinners, one at lunchtime and one in the evening. Cooking and eating hot meals is really important for me. I love my food piping hot, even on the warmest days – no salads for me! Eating chocolate biscuits is fine, if I have had my potatoes, veg, fruit and meat. If I go two or three days eating too much bread, or stuff from the deli counter, I start to feel rotten. It messes with my digestive system. It messes with my energy levels. If I am eating well, everything works better. I work better.

With the weight on there are repercussions and the worst is tiredness. If I spend the day having scones and croissants and sandwiches, I feel tired, and then I reach for a chocolate bar. That happened to me the other day, but when I ate the chocolate bar I found in the fridge I decided the only way out of feeling sluggish was to go to the gym, so I did. That hour and a half in the gym changed my mindset again completely.

As a young fella I slept like a log, but I realise now how little I slept, or how often my sleep was disturbed, once I got into business. I was regularly only getting two or three hours' sleep, and that's harmful both physically and mentally. Sleep is such a key building block for health. Since the accident my nerve pain – and my dogs – will always stop me getting uninterrupted sleep, but I treasure every minute I do get, and I use rest to restore me when I can't have sleep.

However, my biggest achievement wasn't getting back on my feet or walking out the doors of the NRH. My biggest achievement has been to rebuild my mental strength, and the greatest progress in rebuilding myself has happened in the last couple of years, since I began dealing with my demons, with the help of psychotherapy. It still amazes me how quickly I switched from being so positive about physical recovery from my injury, to being so destructive that I wanted to take my own life. I never saw that I was diving towards the bottom, only that I'd reached it. As I was holding on to my physical progress to keep myself positive, I didn't let myself engage with the mental and emotional repercussions of my accident, or the mental health legacy of those years before the accident. Even at the time I knew that it wasn't just my physical body that needed repair. However, I felt I hadn't the energy or the means to deal with anything else – while hoping that eventually I would. I was just trying to get through each day, each week, not realising that by pushing my mental and emotional issues away, I was diving into a darker and darker place.

Accepting I needed help was the first brick I lifted to rebuild that particular wall. The second was taking it and spending a week in a psychiatric ward. Being allowed to talk and think, having no phone to distract me, cleared my head and helped me figure out how important relationships are to me; how I need to challenge myself and create internal competition to keep motivated.

Learning about myself, and understanding what makes me tick, has helped me lay small blocks into my days that contribute to keeping me on an even keel, make me more productive, and lift me back up when I am low. I might notice I am feeling down, and realise I didn't have my cold shower, or didn't make the bed, or haven't been outside for a walk. If I am not meeting a friend, or giving a talk, I drop into a local coffee shop, to sit for a while, just to be social, to have human interaction.' I have discovered that these are all things I need to do to keep myself on an upwards trajectory.

A morning and evening routine puts me on the right track. When I get out of bed, I make it straight away. I feel the day is off to a good start when I do that. I love having everything in its place and tidy. Before a cold shower I'll take my medication with a pint of water, to begin the day hydrated.

In the evening I prepare everything for the following day. I check and iron my clothes. I get my rucksack packed. If I'm prepared I'm able to relax more and tune out. I can't relax if I don't have everything ready, because I know that could mean unexpected stress in the morning. Being prepared removes any potential for stress.

Any bit of exercise is good for my mental health, keeps me mobile and active. If I don't exercise for three days, I'll definitely start feeling down. I no longer find walking hard exercise, but when I work out, I work out really hard. I go to the gym at least four evenings a week.I don't see the point of going and not pushing myself as far as I can. If I went up to the gym and did a half-arsed session, it would be counter-productive. I'd actually feel worse afterwards. It's about pushing my performance. When I am in the gym I do an hour of weights, and I put myself under so much pressure I can't think about anything else.

Exercise and training have been crucial blocks in rebuilding and maintaining my mental health. Exercise also served as a distraction, allowing me to find some quiet time to break out of the cycle of negative thoughts that feed depression. However, after the accident I became very good at using physical exertion to hide or mask my mental state. When I have a physical element I can latch on to, I tend to focus on putting my body through the paces and ignoring my mind. I need to constantly watch that I do not let this happen again or the solid foundations I have rebuilt for myself will crumble.

Allowing myself to be rebuilt meant that I had to redefine my concept of masculinity. I had to realise that showing my weaknesses and my vulnerability, and asking for help, actually made me a stronger and braver man. Being afraid to show any sort of weakness or emotion is what drove me to the edge. I discovered the amount of anguish a man can put himself through before he gets to not wanting to be any more. I am forever thankful that I was stopped before I ended my life, but I know how much a man can swallow up, and pretend that nothing is wrong. When there is a tragedy, when a man takes his own life, people will always say, 'I never saw that coming.' But that's because we are so good at hiding stuff.

I have always been a talker, but not always when I needed to be. I struggle with communication, shutting down rather than having it out or explaining what is bothering me, but I am trying to be more open. It was counselling, talking therapy, that gave me the final tools I needed. And the tools I discovered when I was down on the floor I still use today, because even on an upward trajectory you are going to have bad days. I also now talk to other men about mental health. The message? You need to drop your mask and ask for help when you need it. You will be surprised at the help that is out there, not just the services and professionals, but the people around you.

Changing my perspective on so many things has been key. Life is a journey, and we as human beings, especially ones who want to really push on, will set a lot of goals and end points on that journey. If we don't get to that end point, we're very quick to see that as a failure, because we haven't achieved it. But now I think: 'Okay, here I am now. And that is where I want to be. But even if I only make it a short distance to where I want to be, I've still made progress.' I look at what I have achieved as a person – physical and mental improvements, experiences, new friendships – rather than what I have yet to achieve. I look at what I have, not what I don't have. I am thankful and grateful for my blessings.

So much I have done in my life has been about earning the respect of my peers, in sport and in business. I still want to be respected, to be seen, to be looked up to as a good example; but by the right people, and for the right reasons, not because of my 'status'. Most of all I want my kids to respect me, and to be proud of me, and to love me.

It is my friends and family who have helped me with so much of the heavy lifting since my accident. I had lost contact with many of my friends, but they came running when I needed them. I've now learned to take time to nurture old relationships and to make new ones. I value my friendships and make more of an effort to meet up. For years I would have been very shut off to making new friends or taking time to get to know people. Now I might reach out to other dads on the sideline or stay in contact with the people I meet at talks, the people I might spend an extra hour with afterwards. I put a lot of value on those meetings and those encounters. In the past I would have been out the door as soon as something was over: 'Goodbye and good luck.' I never had time. Being social suits me so much better now.

By being more social I have met some wonderful and interesting people, some who have also undergone life-changing experiences. Through my talks I have been asked to meet other people with acquired disabilities who might be struggling. I am always happy to do that, because I know I have as much to learn from them as they have from me. I appreciate that only someone without the use of some of their bodily functions can understand the struggle that every day brings. Being more social, chatting to people I meet in my day, has also brought chance new connections, and even found me the latest addition to my household – Newfoundland puppy Tiny.

I admire people who love life, who are optimistic, people who really want to make the most of their life, make the most of the now, and make the most of what's presented to them rather than complaining about it. My dad is like that, and I would aspire to be like that too. However, I can still be wobbly, both physically and mentally. If I were a building I would have a lengthy snag list of things that need doing, and that may never be quite done!

I let anger simmer for a long time, and that just sapped my energy, drained my drive. I used sport as a release for anger when I was a younger person. I never felt I was bullied about my size, or let it sit with me. I would go out on the rugby pitch and vent all that frustration. So when I gave up sport, it wasn't scoring a try that I missed. I missed the big hit and the big tackle, clobbering into someone. That released the frustration within me. I looked for other things to find that release, like golf. But there's no frustration released there, it's the other way around.

I've mellowed a lot now, but I think for a few years after giving up rugby, I was really struggling. Looking back, I know that when the business became stressful, it would have been good for me to have had a release like rugby gave me. I am getting better at managing anger. I try not to allow it in, or to sit with me. Keeping stress out of my life, by delegating, by not rushing, by doing things properly the first time, by being prepared, by dealing with problems straight away, helps me to do that. I'm probably not as quick to react, or over-react, when people annoy me. I am definitely calmer. I've learned that if I just let things go, I never explode. I try not to carry things with me. I don't stress about the past, and I don't worry about the future. It's what I do right now that is important.

There are times when that ratty side of me begins to show again. Then I have to ask myself, 'How do I want to be viewed?' 'Is this way of behaving something that I would want my kids to see?' And I do have to say that to myself sometimes. I'll be agitated over something and I'll start to respond angrily. Then I remind myself that the person I'm directing that anger towards has other things going on in their world. Most people don't set out to be mean; everyone has stuff going on, and by giving them grief I'm only making their life worse. I've even managed to get calmer in my approaches to people who park in designated disabled spaces, needed by wheelchair users, a pet hate of mine. If only they realised how lucky they are not to need to park there.

I marvel sometimes now at how much enjoyment I can get out of smaller moments in my day, moments I was never mentally present for in the past, something as simple as buying my kids a hot chocolate and watching the unique ways they all drink it!

Being thankful for what I have, and not worrying about what I don't have, is why I'm so happy now. I know people talk behind my back about where and how I'm living, but I'm content. Because that's not what's important to me in life any more. I want my few comforts. I like a clean and tidy home. But I'm not wrapping myself in a quarter of a million of debt to look good.

Now, even though I'm dealing with the pain and the other effects of my injury, I'm enjoying life. I'm living life. I won't say I'm a different person, but I'm rebuilding the person I should have been.

I am still rebuilding constantly. When I put one stone in place incorrectly, or something throws me off, I collapse a little again. A sense of failure, of not being good enough, has been what has kept me from completing my inner wall. Every now and then that undermines me again. But at least I know now why I can feel the way I do, why it gets to me, and I am finally beginning to accept that it is not true.

HOW TO REBUILD.

Find the building blocks you need to rebuild yourself as a better man or woman. Get help with the heavy lifting. Find ways to release anger and tension that are not destructive for you or those around you. Find joy in the small pleasures.

30

MANUAL FOR A BETTER MAN

As my sons and daughter grow up I find myself wanting to be a better man for them, and this has made me reflect on what I think makes a good man. It's just my opinion, and it's evolving all the time.

I'm still very much a traditionalist. I think a man should provide security for the people around him, that they should feel safe around him. He should be able to provide a living, provide a shelter, make a home. I believe in chivalry, holding doors open, pulling out chairs. I see that as manners, as respect, but I think young lads nowadays are worried about what reaction they might get if they show those manners.

However, my thinking has changed about what makes a strong man. I used to believe that men should not display weakness or show vulnerability. It was our job to fix, to sort, and never to share the burden. Now I know men need to understand that both weaknesses and strengths are part of our make-up and character. And we are all different in that make-up. Our weakness could be somebody else's strength, and that somebody might be right beside us, ready to lend a hand.

Know your limitations, and play to your strengths. If you are not the smartest person in the world, that's through no fault of your own. We are all different. Some people are academic, some people are physically strong. It's easy to know and play to your strengths, but it's really our weaknesses that we need to understand more, so we can improve and thrive.

My message at many of my talks is a simple one, but it can seem incredibly daunting for many people, especially men. Asking for help when we need it is the bravest, strongest and smartest thing you can do. If you were the captain of a sports team, and your team was doing well, think about what would happen if you suddenly stopped training yourself, stopped preparing, and started partying before games. As your standards started to fall, your team would be left without a good leader, without someone they could trust or rely on. They'd have to work extra hard to fill the void that you were leaving. I feel that is like a man who doesn't look after his own mental health and strength and wellbeing. Everything around him is affected, and the people around him, his family, also begin to suffer. So asking for help is the smartest move you can make. It is a sign of strength, not weakness. Mental strength is putting your hand up when you're in trouble. In a man's world, that is the hardest thing to do, but it is about the bravest a man can be.

Men today are torn, and confused, by what they view as the expectations of society, or their peers: winning the big corporate job; driving a top-of-the-range car; owning a big house; going on 'Insta-moment' holidays; having the perfect body; showing off an attractive partner. So-called social influencers drive me cracked. Everyone is aiming for a six-pack, though probably less than 1 per cent of the world's male population under the age of 25 have one. Who decided this is essential to be considered the 'perfect specimen' of manhood? It baffles me. Everyone sees the end results, the 'moment', on social media. What we don't see is what the guy has really had to put himself through to look like that, what he hasn't been able to eat, how miserable he is. What we don't see is that the person with the big house, expensive cars and fancy holidays could be millions in debt and has no time or freedom.

We also don't see the hard work, the sacrifices that have to be made, for athletes to have their 'moments'. No one saw the hard work that it took to get myself through the doors of the NRH, and back through them as a walker and a runner.

Boys need to be true to themselves, not what they think an attractive man looks like. I'd be considered 'masculine' because I am a big strong guy, despite any disability I have. However this is a very shallow view of masculinity. I dislike the word 'macho' because I see that as being almost aggressively manly, showing no signs of weakness, a sort of caricature. The word tends to be attached to big men, who might be gentle giants, rather than the smaller man, no matter how evil and aggressive he is. I am an aggressive person when it comes to sport, but nowhere else.

I accept now that I am an emotional human who needs affection and warmth in his life. I get upset when I see a hurt animal. I cried watching *Remember the Titans* and *Notting Hill*, and Rory McIlroy achieving his goal of winning the US Masters and the Grand Slam. My son Bradley is emotional like me, and I don't tell him not to be, whereas my dad would have told me to 'cop on'. When Bradley's getting very upset over something very small, I might tell him to put his reaction into perspective, that what he's upset about really isn't that important. But then, I have to remind myself, what may not seem important to me is important to him. Boys and young men need to take time to figure out what makes them happy, to be comfortable in their own skins, and not pretend to try and fit in. You only need to be the best version of yourself. Do not accept what other people are telling us a modern man needs to be, including those who preach misogyny.

I'm not comfortable with some role reversals – I like to be the one driving the car – but I'm very happy with others. Currently in our house it is my daughter Aimee who is the sporty one, and she is so good at anything she tries. Twenty years ago girls barely had sports teams. My parents never forced sport on me, and I don't want to force it on my children, even though I know what huge benefits it can bring, and I love to see them all getting involved.

Sport is a great educator and leveller. Maybe I am being simplistic, or naive, but I think that many rural lads find their idols among the local hurlers or footballers or rugby players. They are not looking at the so-called status of money or power, or the toxic male 'influencers'.

Having good character, and doing nobody wrong intentionally, is far more important than status. Because I found such a home in sport, I find it really distressing and disturbing to hear about sexual assaults and rapes in the world of sport, or even see the lack of respect that can be displayed towards women. These are not men to look up to and admire. They don't represent the men I know or would want to know, never mind seeing them held up as heroes.

I want my kids to grow up to be good men and women, with respect, not for the influencers who don't deserve it, but for the elderly, for teachers, for gardaí, for the volunteers, for those who overcome daily struggles, for anyone who is trying to make society a better place, who is trying to live a good life. I want them to live good lives. Men today are struggling with the distorted expectations of society, or their peers. We would all like to be the Rolls-Royces of this world, but 99.9 per cent of us aren't. However, it is the 99.9 per cent of us who actually drive this world forward. We need to be proud of everything we do, if we give it our best. We all need to be better men, and to raise better men.

31

LOOKING AHEAD

Leaving the NRH, the mental lift on the back of my physical gains was massive. I remember saying, 'I'm going to start living my life, start enjoying my life.' I made a sort of bucket list in my head, and that list was mainly about travelling, which is a huge passion of mine, and doing more things with the kids, including travelling with them. I keep a large map of the world on the wall, with pins in all the places I have been. There are quite a lot of pins already, but I want there to be more. Bradley is always looking at it and has told me he wants to go to Germany or London next. I also wanted to get back to my roots, to enjoy more rugby. I wanted to go on a third Lions tour. I wanted to read more books. I wanted to learn a language.

Everything I put on that list was about enjoying life more, having experiences. Nothing has changed since 2019. What I have taken away completely from my wish list are materialistic things, aside from a decent car and money to travel. I just want to enjoy life with my family and friends.

I began travelling as soon as I could after getting out of the NRH, and I now spend a lot of time looking at where I can go next, and how to get there, and then looking at the bank balance and realising I can't afford it! I would really love to get to South America, to Argentina and Patagonia. I have been on safaris in South Africa, but if I had the chance I'd love to go and see tigers in India, or orangutans in their natural habitat. It's not much more difficult to travel now than it was before my accident. I just have to make sure I keep up with my medication and manage my pain as best as I can, and that I don't overdo it. I have adapted to my disability. I just always make sure I have a spare pair of underwear, socks and wipes.

I want to spend more time in nature, explore nature in other countries. I would like to do more hiking. I want to climb Kilimanjaro, and hike in the Italian Dolomites. However, because of my balance issues I know I can't risk taking on bigger challenges on my own in case of an accident.

When people ask me what I do, I'm now very comfortable saying I am a keynote speaker who delivers motivational talks on the importance of health and safety to companies and organisations, and a mental health and disability advocate. More recently, in addition to giving talks, I do the occasional bus job for operators around my area, which I love. That's something I had stopped getting pleasure out of when I was an owner. Then, when I was driving a bus, I was always firefighting, dealing with problems elsewhere, thinking of what had to be sorted, what had to be arranged for the next day, and the day after that, and the day after that. Now, when I drive a bus I can completely block everything else out, I'm just enjoying the journey. And because it's not my vehicle or my customers, I'm far calmer dealing with people who get rowdy or start throwing things about. I'm not on edge the whole time.

I love driving. It's all automatic. I just use my right foot. A lot of the large coaches have a retarder, a hand-controlled engine brake that slows down the vehicle before you have to use the brake. A good driver will always use the engine break because it's more fuel-efficient. Driving is another way to occupy my mind, so if somebody rings me up and I have nothing on, I'll jump at the offer. It's work. It's meeting new people. It's socialising. When I was the boss I never fully engaged with passengers because I was always having to deal with something else, a breakdown or scheduling, or some other fire to put out. Now that I have none of those responsibilities, none of those headaches, I have great chats with people. They go and play their match, and I'll go off for a long walk. I get my exercise in. I do the job and I get paid. I get to socialise. I get to occupy my time. It's a win–win for me, and there is zero stress because I like driving.

I've done a few hiking tours, and I particularly enjoy those because you drive to the location, drop the hikers off, and pick them up five hours later a few miles down the road. Some drivers hate doing those trips because of the long wait and because the tips aren't great, but I love them because I get to do my own exercise and I'm not worried about tips, they're just a bonus. I'm already getting paid for the job. Hikers are usually lovely people, and it's often older European couples on these tours. I wake up in the morning, get out of a bed that I don't have to make, hop into a shower that I don't have to clean, get a breakfast made and put in front of me that I don't have to pay for, or clean up after; and then I start doing the job. Along the way I'll get a free tea or coffee, and a free lunch, and I'll finish the day with a good dinner before hopping into another new bed ... and there's often a gym in the hotel I can go to. So what's not to like? I don't do long trips away because of the kids, but when they are in college or working, I can see myself going off on tours for weeks. That could be a good life.

Since the accident, I can't handle stress, so I keep it out of my life as much as possible. That's another reason why I exercise most days. I don't ever want to go back into a situation where I have employees, or I am managing a company, managing massive debt. Anything I buy these days I pay for up front. I will never borrow money again, aside from a car loan, since a car is essential for me. I will never again get to a place where I am working so hard I am sacrificing or jeopardising the important things in life: time with my family; my health. If I do that I know I'll hit rock bottom again.

I know that because I fear loneliness so much that I would like to be in a relationship again, eventually. My disability doesn't rule out having an intimate relationship. But I'm very happy right now. I'm at my happiest since my accident and my marriage break-up. What's most important to me now is giving my time to my children, continuing to improve my own mental and physical health while working as a mental health and disability advocate, and building on the other relationships in my life.

I have learned as I rebuilt myself that it is challenges that define me, keep me focused and give me a purpose. However, I have also learned that they need to be challenges that I am in control of, that are within my boundaries and my means to complete. I have almost always been a self-employed person, somebody who just grabs things and goes with them, and controls them from start to finish. It may not have always worked out, but I know now that I am happiest when I am pursuing my own goals.

One goal is to set up a mental health roadshow that would travel around to schools and colleges. I would like it to explore the importance for us all of figuring out who we are and staying true to that; to teach how to build up the mental muscle that we need to keep our minds healthy; and to help people understand that their own mental health is at the core of everything – relationships, careers, living a full life. But that is something for the future.

For the moment I am looking at something that will: severely test my endurance; bring awareness to the implications of spinal cord injuries; highlight the mental strength that is needed to get up and keep fighting every day to overcome disabilities; and show what can be achieved against the odds, when you never give up on yourself.

I tried to end my own life when I gave up on myself. The minute you give up on yourself, you could find yourself in a deep dark hole, one that requires huge mental strength to get out of. But it is possible. Inch by inch, we can all get ourselves back out of those depths of despair. Give up on yourself and you never will.

When I began looking at what I would do next, I asked myself why I was really doing another challenge. I'd be doing it to raise money for people who find themselves in difficulties because of a disability, to make my kids proud, and to raise awareness.

So in 2026 I intend to walk across America, 4,500km from Brooklyn in New York to Santa Monica in California. The aim is to raise as much as possible for Spinal Injuries Ireland and generate awareness about spinal cord injuries, including the mental health challenges that can accompany one. I'm told that I will be the first Irishman since 1910 to walk across America, when John Ennis, a Longford man, walked from Coney Island to San Francisco. I will also be the first person with a spinal cord injury to undertake the walk. My route will take me across 13 states: New York, New Jersey, Pennsylvania, West Virginia, Ohio, Indiana, Illinois, Missouri, Kansas, Colorado, Utah, Arizona and California. I'm going to have advice from a nutritionist and a sports scientist when I start training. And I plan to do some of that training along different stages of Ireland's Wild Atlantic Way. That coastline on our tiny island is 2,600km, more than half the distance of coast-to-coast America. I'm hoping that walking through bad weather and on bad roads will help build the body resilience, the store of stamina, that I will need in the US.

In America I will walk 60km a day, the equivalent of a marathon and a half a day, over 75 days, but we have a 90-day window. I will have a support car with me, and people will be invited to fundraise and join me along the route for five days at a time. This challenge is all about getting it done, not setting a time. If the nerve pain gets too much along the route I can pause. I also know that for my body to accomplish a challenge like this I need my sleep, so I'm going to have a bed every night. I need to be social – there will be chats and laughs along the way. I need proper nutrition – I will have good food.

I said in Tomek's documentary that 'When you set your objectives and you don't achieve your objectives, to me, that's still a failure.' I don't believe that now. If I do this walk and I fall and break my leg, or if something else happens that's out of my control, that's something that can't be helped. I don't like failing, but if I let fear of failure keep a hold on me, I would never try anything new, never push myself out of my comfort zone again.

This walk is, once again, about showing people what they can do if they apply themselves and train properly. I want to raise awareness of what can be possible. I still get gripped by guilt that I am walking while so many spinal cord injury patients aren't, but I am trying to use my story to help others.

There are people who will say, 'Sure he's on his feet, what would he know about spinal cord injuries?' They are not the people I am doing this for. I am doing it for the people who find themselves starting their journey with a spinal cord injury, or who want to at least attempt to try new things.

It is only when something is taken away from you that you realise how valuable it is. I take on challenges to try and show people that you are the only person who can help you regain even a little of what you have lost. You will have physiotherapists and occupational therapists and doctors around to support you, but if you don't want to do it, they're not going to force you.

My accident in October 2018 isn't something I have ever felt uncomfortable talking about. It doesn't feel like a traumatic moment, though it was. It's the panic of lung clots, and the pain of the gallstones, and the mental anguish, and the ongoing nerve pain that I find more difficult to discuss or revisit.

However, I'm still living off that moment when I picked up that bench. Everything that has happened, the walk, the row, the run, the talks, the book, are because of that moment. But maybe it will soon be time to reset my life again. At some stage in the future, maybe after the trans-America challenge, it may be time to start living from that new moment, to do something that has nothing to do with my accident, or my injury; to leave it behind me and to forge my next path.

After the walk I will only be 47. I will always set myself challenges, but potentially this next walk could be my final, though lasting, imprint on the world of spinal cord injuries. I don't know how I will be thinking when it is over, but I hope that whatever I do in the future, whatever legacy I create, I will leave a positive imprint on the world around me. I would be happy with that.

My message is not just for people with spinal cord injuries. It is for anyone who has been injured, disabled – acquired or otherwise – sick, who has suffered the after-effects of a stroke or other health setback, and is struggling mentally and physically because of the condition they find themselves in. It is also for the fully able-bodied who are not fulfilling their full potential.

It is also a message to those who plan and provide our services. Isolation undermines the efforts of anyone who is trying to recover. If someone cannot get up and out to shop, or to a restaurant or gym, or a class, their world shrinks. We are social animals and the more difficult we make it for people with disabilities, either physical or mental, to feel part of the social fabric that surrounds them, the more likely it is they will stay at home and regress. We are not here just to exist, to survive; we are here to live, and live well.

Every day is a day to improve for all of us. Just trying can make us feel more positive. Your walk will be different from mine. Your path will be different from mine. My new goal is to walk across America. Your goal might be to walk across the corridor, or to train for a 5k, or just move a finger. It's not about getting up on your feet and walking, it's about pushing yourself as hard as you can, to find out what is possible for you.

LIFE IS ABOUT THE JOURNEY, NOT THE OUTCOME. IT'S PROGRESS, NOT FAILURE.

Success isn't just about the end result; it's about the journey. And that journey lasts as long as we are alive. Failure is something that hits me hard, but I know now that if I don't achieve my goal I will still have improved along the road.

If you train for a marathon but don't make the finish line, that doesn't mean failure. You are now a healthier, fitter person than you were before you started training. Missing the finish line is just part of the journey. There is beauty, and progress, in every journey we take during our lives, no matter the outcome.

ACKNOWLEDGEMENTS

MY FAMILY

Dad, for being my rock at all times.
Mom, for taking on all the stress and worries of the world on to herself.
My sister Attracta, for always wanting the best for me.
Derek, Kathleen and Eoin Caulfield for supporting me when it matters most.

MY KIDS

Aimee, Bradley and Felim, for being the reason to keep on fighting, and bringing joy to the simple things in life. I LOVE YE.

I would also like to acknowledge that my kids are blessed to have a fantastic mother. Thank you, Mandy, for bringing them into our world.

FRIENDS

I'm blessed with great friends from the Athenry and rugby communities. You all know what you have done for me over the years. It will never be forgotten. It has been a rollercoaster full of amazing memories with many more to come.

MEDICAL WORLD

Paramedics, A&E team, Mater Hospital National Spinal Injury Unit, St Finbar's Ward in University Hospital Galway, National Rehabilitation Hospital, Psychiatric Ward in University Hospital Galway – without the care of the people in all these places and their dedication to what they do, I would not be here today, on my own two feet. THANK YOU.

CHALLENGES AND FUNDRAISERS

A massive thank you to all the sponsors who help to get each project up and running and helped raise much-needed money for some truly worthy charities. Thank you also to all the people who gave their free time to make each project a success. Without you, nothing would ever have happened.

PROJECT EMPOWER

Thank you, Damo, for giving me the opportunity to row the North Atlantic Ocean. I have some incredible memories and life lessons from the experience. Thanks to Paul Cleary in New York for everything he did for me after my rescue. Thanks to David McCormack for looking out for me while I was in New York. Top man.

To Tomek Ciezki from Heavy Man Films, Boyd Challenger and Emilija Jefremova, who all helped visually document the story of Project Empower. Thank you.

Thanks to Captain Sanjay Karki and his crew from Hafnia Shenzhen, who rescued me from the Gulf Stream.

Thanks to Justin Adkin, who built the most amazing and safe boat in which to row the North Atlantic Ocean and to Chris Martin for his on ground support during the row.

CHARITIES/ ORGANISATIONS/ COMPANIES

Thank you all for having faith in me to deliver talks to your teams in the hope they will create long lasting and meaningful impact. I have never enjoyed doing something as much as what I do now. I'm truly passionate about it. It's amazing what happens when you take one step at a time.

GILL BOOKS

Without Gill Books belief in me, and without all their amazing team, this book would not be possible. Thank you for giving me this once-in-a-lifetime opportunity.

WRITER

Lastly, a massive thank you to Louise Ní Chríodáin, who guided me through the process with great passion and care, and got the most out me.